WITH MALICE TOWARD SOME

MARGARET HALSEY

With Illustrations by
PEGGY BACON

SIMON AND SCHUSTER
New York · 1938

PART I

Arrival

Getting married was nothing. I had the German measles on my wedding day and a raging temperature, so that I was married under forced draught, as it were, and afterwards I went back to bed and opened a fresh box of Kleenex. That seems a long time ago. But now Henry has an exchange professorship for next winter at a small college in Devonshire, and we are sailing on the *Britannic* tomorrow for twelve months in Europe. Henry is tranquil. He has been to Europe several times before and is by nature as unruffled as a dish of Jello in a flat calm. But I have never traveled, and the suitcases and tissue paper and coathangers have wrought me to such a white heat of excitement that I could be put on an anvil and hammered into any shape you want.

The incredible moment when the boat first began to move past the pier is over and done with by several hours now and I am left feeling, to tell the truth, rather flat and disheartened. Nothing, I suppose, will ever seem quite so miraculous again, and how am I to get through the long, tepid vista of the rest of my life? But Henry says that people who have been to Europe do manage somehow, and occasionally even show a degree of enthusiasm for living to ripe old ages. He submits that I am over-tired and handsomely offers, if I will take a nap before dinner, to read me to sleep.

We are having a storm, and the *Britannic* has spent two days trying to conclude a working agreement with the Atlantic Ocean and failing miserably. Henry's stomach and mine are both behaving like perfect little ladies and, as a matter of fact, I rather like that long, powerful, upward swing and the creaking, downward plunge. But it is not everybody's motion and the boat has a horribly front-line-trenches atmosphere about it. By a series of experiments, I have discovered that the bar is the safest place for a person who has any lingering fondness for human dignity and they will have to hew me out of it when we get into smooth water again. Henry, however, roves around at will. I should not like to call him insensitive, but it is my private opinion that he must have nerves like hawsers.

June 3rd

The sun has come out again and there is only a little swell.

June 5th

We have been reading and getting sunburned and playing Russian Bank together and Henry is still in the Ping-pong tournament. The other passengers consist of some priests and nuns; some old men who drink extensively but without flair; a handful of harassed, pathetic fathers and mothers who peer shudderingly down the ventilators in search of missing children; and a large group of beautiful, shiny-looking young people who generally travel about in a flying wedge and whose voices are distressingly reminiscent of seagulls discovering floating orange peel. We have not talked very much with these citizens, as most of the secular ones seem to be in the midst of an impromptu mating season. When we do have a few exchanges with them, they always tell Henry, on finding out that he is a teacher, that he would not believe the books they read, psychology. Under any other circumstances I would be inclined to call them dull, but as it is, my heart is too full of gratitude toward them for being well again.

Later

Henry has been eliminated from the Pingpong tournament by a gigantic blond Englishman who is returning from Zanzibar and who is referred to by everyone, with the possible exception of the stewards, as the Post of Empire.

June 6th

The boat gets in tomorrow and we have been talking about our summer plans, though without arriving at any very definite conclusions. Henry is not one to tug and shove at plans and arrangements just for the exercise, being divinely tall and most divinely laissez-faire, and I have picked up something of the same attitude —partly from sheer propinquity and partly from observing that things seem to turn out all right for Henry anyway, even though he does not bother to give them any encouragement. We have to go to Exeter after we land, so that Henry can meet his future colleagues and we can find some place to live in this winter, but when that is done, we have the whole summer before us. One thing is certain, and that is that we want to spend part of it in Norway and Sweden.

While Henry has gone to buy chocolate bars and reading matter, I am sitting in the waiting room of the Southampton station of the Southern Railway. My eyes, I am afraid, are going to fall right out of their sockets before the end of the day—I have been looking at everything so strenuously. It took a long while to get off the boat, and involved a great deal of standing in line and filling out cards and blanks. There is something about filling out printed forms which arouses lawless impulses in me and makes me want to do things that will have the file clerks sitting up with a jerk, like putting in

RELIGION......*Druid*......

Today, when one of my blanks said OCCUPATION, I wrote down *none*, though I suspected this would not do. A severe but courteous official confirmed this impression. So I crossed it out and wrote *parasite*, which, not to be too delicate about it, is what I am. This made the official relax a little and he himself put *housewife* in what space there was left. "Be a prince," I said. "Make it *typhoid carrier*." But he only smiled and blotted out *parasite* so that it would not show.

It is a grey day and all around the docks was a landscape of engine grease and smoke. Nevertheless, whoever it was that said not Angles, but angels, must have been talking about English porters, customs men and railroad attendants. They have been taking care of us with a solicitude you could not hope to receive in the United States unless you were either the President or noticeably pregnant. The porters did not look at their tips, only smiled and raised their caps. I half expected them to say if they had known we were coming, they would have whipped up a cake.

Later

Still in the railroad station. The Southern Railway, not used to being confronted with people who want to go from Southampton to Exeter, is still rummaging good-naturedly in its bureau drawers, trying to see whether it can rig up something. Meanwhile, we have been for a walk around some of the streets of Southampton. How *small* everything is! The automobiles are like toys, there are no apartment buildings (at least, I did not see any), and everybody appears to live in a tiny little house with a tiny little garden in front. The older-looking streets are so narrow that evidently only the car tracks keep them from closing up altogether. Two things that surprised me: the small, shabby and ineffectual-seeming business buildings, with their shopwindows like mangers, and the way in which things are growing—and growing with what might almost be called abandon—on every spot of ground big enough to drop a handkerchief on.

Today is Sunday, and the English Sunday has started right in to live up to what I had read about it. Everything is closed up, the streets are empty, and the citizens have all gone down into their cellars and pulled pillowcases over their heads. I keep having an impulse to go up to one of those sealed front doors, tap on it and say politely, "May I suggest a raven?"

This seems to be a day for waiting rooms. We are at Salisbury now, with three hours to wait before the Exeter train is due. Everything would be all right, it seems, if only we were going *to* London instead of away from it. But English trains apparently make a habit of always going toward London, and when they get there, are taken apart and mailed back to Land's End and Edinburgh. I am partial to them, nevertheless. The locomotives are only about thirty-four inches around the bust, but they can and do pull a string of cars at eighty miles an hour. And I like the compartments. There was no one in ours from Southampton to Salisbury, and I felt at once snug and opulent, like a chocolate in a weekend package.

The train to Exeter will be here in twenty-five

minutes now. Meantime, much encouraged by the sun's suddenly coming out brilliantly, we have been to look at Salisbury Cathedral. In Southampton England seemed a whittled-down little country, but in Salisbury it seems hoary and impressive. A lawn with grass growing on it like fur lies next to the Cathedral. Around the lawn is a low stone wall, bordered with flower beds. When I was a child, my father was enthusiastic about gardening and my first youthful contact with reality was the unavoidable conclusion that Father's nasturtiums were pretty niggardly affairs compared with the pictures in Peter Henderson's catalogue. (As a matter of fact, this sad discrepancy struck Father rather forcibly too, and in the end he gave up gardening and moved into an apartment.) But when I saw the flowers in the Cathedral Close at Salisbury, I realized what Peter Henderson had had in mind. Apparently it is possible, in England, actually to achieve those burning phalanxes of bloom that used to be so nobly illustrated between the end of Grass Seed and the beginning of Hardy Perennials.

We walked around at a slow, ecclesiastical pace, while I looked about me and tried to feel equal to my surroundings. They were unbelievably pictorial—heavy trees and grey ranks of pointed arches; the lawn green in the sunlight with a full-blooded, lambent greenness such as I have never seen in America; the Cathedral tower holding itself up against the moving clouds; and the flower borders bravely being *gemütlich* in the teeth of all the ancestral grandeur. Some dozen or two choir boys in grey robes and white collars were scouring the plain with their Chaucerian draperies tucked into their pants pockets. Whether because it was Sunday or because they were under the influence of the churchly atmosphere, their noise sounded more temperate than boys' racket generally does. A portly old cleric in a wide-brimmed hat coasted out from behind a buttress, and the choristers magically coagulated into a double line and marched off, demure but glistening with perspiration.

Entering the Cathedral, I found myself confronted with two factors I had not counted upon. One was that for all the sunlit splendor of the exterior, the inside was morbidly, icily damp. The other was the unnerving discovery that if you tiptoe through a cathedral you feel sheepish and silly, but if you do not, you feel like a boor. However, there is a bumper crop of dead knights in Salisbury, and I enjoyed myself. Mine is not a tender nature, and ordinarily there is the same amount of sentiment in my disposition that there is in Caesar's *Commentaries*, but I have a sense of the past which could be laid out flat and made up into awnings. There is no stained, battered, worn-down, gouged-out, hard-featured chair or table I will not have a fondness for, if I am assured it is an antiquity, and to stand on a piece of pavement which is being held up by the three remaining handfuls of Jane Austen or Edward the Confessor seems to me a breath-taking privilege. Then, too, it is fortifying to wander around among knights in effigy who look much the same, though they may have breathed their last two hundred years apart, or to examine recumbent stone bishops who have been giving up the ghost with pious regularity from the thirteenth century to the day before yesterday. It makes dying lose its customary aspect and begin to seem merely a slight but universal weakness, like catching cold.

We are in Exeter, established in one of the dormitories—hostels, they call them here. It is more than bedtime, and I am so sleepy I hardly dare look in a mirror, for fear of discovering that my eyes have melted and run together, but I am reluctant to go to bed and bring this day to a close. The English countryside, as we saw it from the train this afternoon, is so intensely rural that it makes the country land-scapes at home seem, in retrospect, faintly ur-ban. The thatched farmhouses are low-slung, and have not only an air of having pushed their way up through the ground, but also an air of being quite ready to push their way back down

12

again. There were no fences, only hedgerows brimming with vines and spouting up occasionally in a small tree. English trees are chubbier than ours. Here and there you see one standing alone in a field, brawny and powerful and immensely historic, with gnarled, rheumatic branches coming out very low down on the trunk. I expected England to be green, but I had not visualized anything so juicily and fervently green as it turned out to be. The country today was grazing rather than farming land. At intervals we passed villages where some of the houses had thatched roofs and some were bricky and bulging with bay windows, but all of them were pastern deep in gardens. For the most part, however, the countryside was prospect succeeding prospect of woodland, streams, hills and meadows—all, evidently, custom-tailored by Alfred Lord Tennyson.

Between Salisbury and Exeter we shared the compartment with a good-humored major of artillery. Gloved, groomed, polished and brushed until he was immaculate as an operating room, he made Henry, who wears the best-cut suit as if it were a toga, look diffuse and shaggy. But next to Henry's long, lean, scholastic features, the major's pink cheeks and bright blank eyes seemed to have been hand-colored by an amateur china painter. He gave us cigarettes (English cigarettes—I can see they are going to take some getting used to) and talked to Henry about India. In India, he said, if you take a rose from your dinner table and stick it in the earth, it will take root and grow. To me, listening with half an ear while I looked out of the window, he sounded wistful about the East. Heat, homesickness and insects figured prominently in his reminiscences, but when he concluded that it was a bit grim, what?, his voice was leaking nostalgia.

June 8th

Today Henry and I and some of the faculty from the college lunched at an Exeter restaurant. It was a bad lunch, half cold and wholly watery, and in order to keep body and soul together, I asked for a glass of milk. The waitress was staggered.

"Milk?" she said incredulously.

"Why, yes," I replied, almost equally incredulously. "A glass of milk."

She wheeled off in the direction of the kitchen. In three minutes she was back again.

"Please," she asked, "do you want this milk hot or cold?"

I blinked a little and said I wanted it cold. The Englishmen who were with us looked amused. "You Americans," one of them said, with a spacious tolerance. We resumed our conversation, and in a short space the waitress made

14

a third appearance. She had a hounded expression.

"Do you," she inquired desperately, "want this milk in a cup or a glass?"

"Just roll it up in a napkin," I answered thoughtlessly, and then was sorry, seeing how embarrassed and confused she was. I started to make amends, but she suddenly bolted and I never saw her again. Another waitress came to take the dessert order and the milk project was tacitly abandoned. I begin to understand the unsavory reputation of English teeth, which—from the little bit I have seen so far—is lamentably well deserved. But one curious point remains unexplained—why are the false teeth so amateurish? They all look as if they had been filched from the Etruscan Room of a museum.

June 9th

I am glad I am coming back to Devonshire this winter and will have a chance to get my mind tidied up about it. All day long I do and see unfamiliar things and everything is so noticeable, by reason of its novelty, that I begin to feel like fresh-laid cement over which cows have been driven. I suppose after a while I will get used to not being used to things.

This hostel at which we are staying is so lovely and so lavish that I would not be surprised to see it all carted away some morning in

15

Metro-Goldwyn trucks. It is an old country house just outside Exeter which the college has only recently acquired. The twenty-odd rooms are skimpily furnished as yet and full of echoes, but the house is plethoric with Adam mantels and the main staircase brings out a touch of the Lady Prioress even in me.

Later

I have to write in snatches, for not only do we go out to lunch and dinner to meet people, but we meet them also at elevenses (which is coffee at eleven o'clock in the morning) and at afternoon tea. The hostel grounds are fully as gentlemanly as the hostel. They extend over fourteen acres, irregular and full of ups and downs, and are planted with patriarchal oaks and old beeches of Falstaffian girth whose lower branches almost touch the grass. Beyond the house is a closed-in garden with fruit trees trained along the walls. In another place, a formal walk of thick-growing English grass leads to clipped yew trees and plantations of rhododendrons, these latter twenty feet high and practically solid bloom. The roses are just coming out, and under the balustrade in front of the house the lilacs are in mid-career. Near the walled garden is a gentle slope which absolutely sputters with flowers—Oriental poppies twice as big as a grapefruit, Canterbury bells, day lilies, lupin, foxglove, peonies, forget-me-not, violets nearly the size of pansies, rock roses, various kinds of daisies, columbine, larkspur and more whose names I do not know. Our window overlooks this Saturnalia of blossom and in the early morning cuckoos sing—or rather, enunciate—in the trees beyond.

Later

Well, to be perfectly frank about it, the disadvantages of English life (which I accepted with such jovial tolerance when I was comfortably reading about them in New York) are beginning to hit a little closer home. It is so damp! I wear a light coat indoors and a heavy one outside, and yet it still seems to me that I can almost feel the mould forming on my face and hands. We are much invited out and we take our meals everywhere—in other hostels, in restaurants and in private houses. I was well warned about English food, so it did not surprise me, but I do wonder, sometimes, how they ever manage to prise it up long enough to get a plate under it. Still, it is very beautiful here, even if it does make a soft, tender New Yorker feel as if he had just been taken out from under glass.

I have been looking for a house. It will have to be a house—there are no small apartments in Exeter, except odd little cul-de-sacs made out of

17

people's old dining rooms—and I think I should like it to be somewhere in the countryside beyond the town. I like the country and I like a good, citified city, like New York, but suburbs and provincial cities (even when, like Exeter, they have a cathedral and a ruined castle) have too much half-wayness about them for my extremist tastes.

June 10th

The college hostels are presided over by Wardens, and the Warden of the one at which we are staying is a woman who is well-connected and exceedingly thankful for it. Through her influence, the wife of a bishop was persuaded, since she happened to be passing through Exeter, to stop off and have tea at the hostel this afternoon. This visit the Warden represented as a great condescension. A bishop's mate is nothing to look down your nose at in any case, and this one is the sole survivor of an ancient race and a titled lady in her own right, her folks having owned and operated Queen Elizabeth and made a very good thing of it. The Warden seemed to think the tea would be a pretty salubrious experience for all us commoners, and I could not shake off the notion that the bishop's wife would look like Vitamin D.

However, she did not look like Vitamin D. She did not, in fact, look like much of anything.

She was of an indefinite age and wore a wrinkled dress of blue voile and a black straw hat shaped like a terminal moraine. You would have taken her for the wife of a chicken farmer, rather than the last of the Warwickshire Mohicans. As she was hard of hearing, the conversation progressed with difficulty. When she had been made to understand that Henry and I were Americans, she asked me what I thought of England. I answered that I thought it was an extremely beautiful country.

"What?" she said.

"It's an extremely beautiful country," I repeated with a great effort at distinctness.

She looked blank. Ten or twelve hand-picked students had been mobilized from various hostels for the tea, so that the fragrance of a two-ply aristocrat should not be wasted on the desert air. One of the young men took up the refrain.

"She says it's an *extremely beautiful* country," he said hardily. There was still no sign of understanding.

The Warden nodded to another student, a girl this time, who rose and went over to the guest. Putting her lips close to the visitor's ear, she declared, "EXTREMELY BEAUTIFUL."

"Ah," said the bishop's mate, and relaxed. She gave me a stately but amiable inclination of the head. Deaf and dowdy as she was, she undeniably had manner, though I think if I had been the Warden and had invited fourteen or so people to an exhibition of pure manner, I would have thrown in somebody who could blow smoke rings, as a makeweight.

We soon gave up trying to include the bishop's lady in the conversation. The students brought her tea, thin bread and butter, jam and cakes, and they took turns timidly lowering themselves down beside her on the sofa and injecting her with a question or a simple comment. This seemed a workable enough arrangement and things went on very satisfactorily, though I was so cold my fingers would not work and my hands moved all in one piece. It had originally been planned to have tea in the grounds. But the day was rainy and wintrily cold, so the ceremony took place indoors in a tall, chilly, beautiful room with no fire in the fireplace and all the windows open.

Henry brought the visitor a second cup of tea.

"In America you don't have tea in the afternoon," she said to him abruptly. Henry shook his head.

"The bishop and I went to America," continued the lady. "They always gave us tea." Henry made a modest clucking sound, as who should say, "Ah, those polite Americans . . . ," but the guest did not hear it. The two of them looked at each other dubiously for a minute and then Henry backed away.

Gradually the students, always well-mannered, lost their frightened look. The Warden, who fancies herself in the rôle of the queenly and well-born hostess, was being gracious on all eight cylinders, and certainly the affair did seem to be going off remarkably well. But suddenly there was a hideous interruption. The distinguished visitor got a crumb in her throat and began to choke terrifyingly. Henry, who tends to be pragmatic, got up to pound the episcopal back. Halfway there, however, he paused, and either losing his nerve or deciding that the lady was not worth saving, he turned around and came back again. This left nothing for the rest of us to do but pretend we did not hear any whooping sounds and act as if at least one death by strangulation were a feature of every well-run tea party. The Warden, a cup of tea in her hand, bent over the gurgling noblewoman, and the rest of us said distractedly that it was frightful weather, oh yes frightful, yes really dreadful.

When the guest had finally managed to get down a swallow of tea and had subsided from purple to an angry pink, the Warden waved to us to go away. We rose gratefully, said good-bye with carefully averted eyes, and filed sheepishly out. Later on, the Warden sought out Henry

21

and me as we were writing letters and talked about the crumb as if it had been planted by Communists, acting under explicit instructions from Moscow.

June 11th

I have not found a furnished house yet, though Henry has nearly finished making his arrangements against the autumn. Where we will go next is still undecided, but he talks of moving on. The difficulty is that there are only two kinds of houses for rent: either family mansions, built in accordance with the British notion that a marriage which is an ounce short of twelve children is a mere liaison; or what the English call "modern villas," which are workingmen's houses and are very tiny, very shiny and furnished throughout in orchid taffeta. Between house-hunting and exposing myself to the benevolent hospitality of the faculty, the days are full, and I find myself getting slightly less conscious of England. I can sometimes climb on a bus without thinking, "This is an English bus," or cross a road without reflecting, "This is an English road." But I do occasionally get a little hungry for sunshine. To this unrelenting raininess, I suppose, Devonshire owes its greenness and its bursting gardens, both very commendable institutions. Now and then, however, I think sadly of the lustrous June weather at home and wonder how I will get along for a whole year in this dim aquarium of a country.

I have a few minutes to write, while Henry gets dressed for dinner. (Henry is subject to brown studies, which usually attack him just as he is about to put his shoes on.) Exeter is beginning to lose its tapestry-like quality and to take shape instead as a city full of human beings. Besides the college, there are some sixty-odd thousand people who support nine moving picture houses. If they do anything else, I do not know what it is, as this part of England is all agricultural. There are no movies on Sunday, owing to the improving influence of the Cathedral. The Cathedral, smaller than the one at Salisbury, is ornate and finely cut and has a delicate majesty, and you would never think to look at it that it lies across the life of the town like Welsh rabbit on a delicate stomach, but so it seems to do. The Cathedral entourage appears to be closely linked up with the well-to-do and influential laity, and I gather that this Holy Alliance is inclined to look with disfavor on the college. By having two or three Socialists on the faculty, the college attains the status of a hot-bed of radicalism, though it certainly does not look to me like a hotbed of anything.

Back from dinner, where I sat next to a young
23

Canadian architect who lives and works in the next county. We got along well. I asked him, in comparing notes on English and American civilization, whether there is much graft in this country. He smiled. "They don't call it graft," he said. "It's all done with so much Old World charm that it's quite painless. The Rape of the Sabine Women set to a minuet."

June 12th

Once you get past the English flavor of things, the pattern of Exeter seems to be much like the pattern of American provincial cities—a large, tame population of movie-goers; a handful of upper-crusters, not so tame; a good library; no music to speak of; and a rather distressing preoccupation with entertaining and being entertained. Physically, though, the city is a thousand times more interesting than its American counterparts. Just off the main street on one side stands the Cathedral, and just off it on the other side is a hill, crowned with a park whose banks of flowers and manicured tidiness make the usual American park look like a bowling alley on Saturday night. The park surrounds some crumbling, reddish walls, remains of a castle built by William the Conqueror, and commands a view over rows and rows of small red-brick houses to the green hills beyond.

24

The main street itself is narrow, swarming with traffic, and lined with hunched-up buildings three or four stories high. Occasionally the round-shouldered ranks of commercial architecture are interrupted by an old Tudor façade, slanting, insecure and quaint, with projecting upper floors. About halfway down the street a clumsy portico, the color of liver and bacon, comes out over the sidewalk. It belongs to the Guild Hall, which dates from the fourteenth century. The citizens of Exeter, I have discovered in my laboratory work, like to have it spoken of with respect.

Notes on a Dinner

1. Henry sitting next to a High Churchwoman who, since she has nothing else to do, makes a career of piety.

   "I often speculate," she said to him provocatively, "on what St. Theresa must have thought of God. A mystic like that."

   "Oh," answered Henry absently, "I guess she liked Him all right."

2. Table d'hôte:

   Canned grapefruit (slightly warmed)
   This is unusual and was probably designed as a sop to the Americans, which is exactly what it was.

Soup

The soup, thin and dark and utterly savorless, tasted as if it had been drained out of the umbrella stand.

Roast beef

The meat is the one bright spot in the local cuisine. It seems a shame to spoil this symmetry of criticism with a word of praise, but I do think English meat much superior to ours, finer textured and with more flavor.

Boiled potatoes and Brussels sprouts

Here is a country where the soil is so fertile that if you plant an acorn in the ground, you have to jump back quickly in order not to have it hit you on the way up. And the English raise Brussels sprouts. Just Brussels sprouts. With sometimes a flyer in cabbage. Is it pure ignorance, or some complicated form of Puritan spitefulness?

Raspberry tart

It is possible to eat English piecrust, whatever you may think at first. The English eat it, and when they stand up and walk away, they are hardly bent over at all. It can be eaten, but it definitely does not come under the head of sensual indulgence.

Savoury

This is a sardine (or, alternatively, a piece of cheese) resting on toast which sweats melted butter. It serves no discernible function except to give the maids another lap to walk.

3. The Warden of our hostel across the table from me, talking to a young Civil Servant about the various aspects and attributes of a local nobleman called Lord Minturn. Judging by the Warden-Servant conversation, if Lord Minturn does not pinch-hit for God in Devonshire, it is only because of manly modesty on his part and not because he is unequal to the task.

"And the little grandson," I heard the Servant exclaim in a rapture of self-abasement.

"Charming," clanged the Warden. "A perfect pet of a child."

"Has the Minturn gingery hair," said the Servant. (For a moment I thought he was going to drop into baby-talk.) "His mother . . ."

The Warden cut him short.

"His mother," she replied, in the tone of one describing something fished up from a manhole, "was an American."

4. The good manners of educated Englishmen, which are the most exquisitely modulated attentions I have ever received. Such leaping to feet, such opening of doors, such lightning flourishes with matches and cigarettes—it is all so heroic, I never quite get over the feeling that someone has just said, "To the life-boats!" Poor Henry cannot keep up with this high-powered chivalry. Despite his being thin as a wand, he is preternaturally slow of movement. I myself always forego his courtesies, not having patience to wait until they ripen and drop from the womb of time, and here, while the Englishmen are fleetly handing around tea or coffee or ashtrays, Henry more often than not is poised in the background looking well disposed but not very well organized.

5. The placid smoothness of English hospitality, which shows up somewhat painfully those American dinners where the best foot is so far forward there is hardly space for anything else in the room.

6. The classics scholar with a crumbled, beautiful face, like a ruined tower, who exorcised the Warden. The Warden has what, with a little cultivation, would be a one-track mind, and she hammered away at Lord Minturn

until there was nothing left of him but shredded pulp.

". . . forty thousand acres," she explained to the table at large, "but one would never know it to see him."

"Did you expect him," asked the scholar mildly, "to have earth under his nails?"

7. The boneless quality of English conversation, which, so far as I have heard it, is all form and no content. Listening to Britons dining out is like watching people play first-class tennis with imaginary balls. No awkward pauses, no sense of strain, mar the gentle continuity of the talk. It goes on and on, effortlessly spinning words and words and yet more words out of the flimsiest material: gardening; English scenery; innocuous news items; yesterday's, today's and tomorrow's weather.

By the time this evening was over, I felt, intellectually, like a baby that is cutting its teeth and has nothing to bite on, but there are two things I like about this verbal thistle-down. It is so skillful and practised, and also so remote and impersonal, that even I manage to hold my own in it—though ordinarily I am stiff-tongued to a degree which makes other guests think I must be one of the host's feeble-minded relatives and tactfully refrain from asking questions about me. Then, too, there is an aura of repose about this sort of conversation. These people do not talk, as so many Americans do, to make a good impression on themselves by making a good impression on somebody else. They have already made a good impression on themselves and talk simply because they think sound is more manageable than silence.

June 13th

I have not only found a house, but I have found a house which qualifies as one of the major satisfactions of life. Henry, who has not seen it yet, says it is rather expensive, but I cannot tell about that. Figures tinkle against my mind and drop off, like gravel hitting a barn door, and financially I live in utter darkness. But Henry is only registering Class B, or Mild-Fatherly objections, not the Class A, They-Shall-Not-Pass type of protest which warns me that I have overshot the mark.

The house is in a village called Yeobridge which dozes primly in the lee of a steep hill, about eight miles from Exeter. A handful of narrow streets with a fair quota of thatched roofs is the nucleus of the village, and the houses of the better-off people are scattered around the outskirts. There are two butcher shops, a post office, and a general store with yokelish green-and-brown sweaters in one window and cheese in the other. Our house is only ten years old, which, down here, is considered brazenly modern. In these parts, it is the ancient things—the worn old churches, the white cottages and the quiet, immemorial lanes—which enjoy all the prestige, and rightly so. The modern aspects of Devonshire civilization are generally only a sluggish imitation of America.

But our house is an exception. A high, moss-encrusted wall, with little ferns growing in the crevices, surrounds the house and only the casement windows of the gables are visible over the top. Inside there is half an acre of English garden with all the habitual picturesqueness of such projects. It includes a grass walk, terminating at each end in two tall evergreen shrubs, slender and dark and Italian-looking. The house stands just where the village street turns into a high-banked lane and curves away out of sight behind an enormous cedar tree. It turns its back on the village, and the principal rooms look down on the garden, the cedar tree and the bend in the road. Beyond the garden is an orchard, and beyond that are assorted Devonshire hills. It is all so attractive, it seems to call for a calendar pasted underneath.

Later

Apropos of the above, I think only the rapidly changing weather saves this sweetly pretty kind of countryside from getting to seem, after a

31

while, like a cheap reproduction. But with all the variations of light, the landscape seldom has the same aspect for two hours together and there is a richness about it which I doubt it would have, in a climate with any pretensions to decency.

June 14th

LIVERPOOL—We are here on a flying trip to meet two American girls, aged sixteen and eighteen—friends of friends of Henry's—who are coming over from New York alone. Apparently the English cook and keep warm entirely with coal fires. I have smelled coal gas in Southampton; in obsolete, non-utilitarian Exeter; even in the streets of country villages where I have been to look for houses. In Liverpool you can almost scoop it up with your hands. And today being Sunday, the town—evidently no *fête champêtre* at best—has put on the air of a person suffering from acute biliousness, complicated by multiple bereavements.

It took us seven hours to get here, for the train padded along like an old woman with a basket on her head. The compartment was crowded all the way. The passengers were not what the English call gentlefolk, but they were uniformly cheerful. They sat uncomplainingly with monolithic suitcases resting on their toes and laughed when their sides were stove in by questing elbows. I admired their hardihood of spirit, though I could have wished them somewhat less hardihood of body. It was raining and the air was more like November than June. At every station Henry wistfully closed the window, and at every station three or four puffing, red-faced Britishers got in, clawed off their coats, said they could not breathe, and opened it again. They had no idea they were being cruel, but by the time we reached Liverpool I was so cold I had to ask Henry please not to knock up against me, or I would chip.

We fumbled blindly for a hotel, and got one that was large, cold, gloomy, sad-colored and disheartening. We have just had dinner to match. Henry has called up the Port Authority and learned that the boat gets in at six o'clock tomorrow morning and that if we do not want to take a chance of missing our babies, we had better be there.

June 15th

Exeter—We got up at five o'clock this morning (which was not much trouble, as the beds were like relief maps) and were down at the dock by six. It was closed up tight. A watchman found us standing dubiously in the sixty-mile gale of wind and rain which was blowing up from the River Mersey. He had a red muffler and the child-like, trusting friendliness that

33

seems to be peculiar to the English lower-income groups. Having taken us into his shack and invited us to warm ourselves at his fire, he went out to see if he could learn when the boat would be in. Not for at least an hour, he said when he came back, and advised us to go around the corner to the Y. M. C. A. and get some coffee.

A wooden building consisting of one room filled with long trestle tables and benches housed the Y. M. C. A. It was bare and dull, but clean. Half a roomful of stevedores and dock workers were eating there. They had pasty faces and in their thick, ill-fitting clothes the wrinkles at elbow and knee had been hollowed out into permanent channels. Every other man had a handle-bar moustache, and they all looked uncompromisingly English. The coffee was grey and I could not drink it, but the men swallowed huge gulps and with it they ate chunks of greyish-looking bread. Some of them smiled at us, but most of them paid no attention.

The boat, ultimately, came in at nine o'clock. In the interval we sat in the Y., and then went back to the dock, where a rusty little man told us that this dock was called Pneumonia Alley, because it was the coldest place in the whole Port of Liverpool. We hastily adjourned to the Y. again. We sat there smoking and not watching the stevedores (though acutely conscious of them) and discussing with sad self-complacency

34

the increasing anomalousness of people like us—
who sit (all starry-eyed and liberal) in fur-lined
academic niches and indulge in the enervating
habit of looking at both sides of things.

The American girls were pretty and animated
and beautifully dressed. Shining with laughter,
the first one hobbled down the gangplank, one
foot blunt in bandages, and stewards clinging to
her, rather than she to them. In her excitement
at getting to Europe, she had fallen downstairs
on the way to breakfast. The other girl got off
the boat unconcernedly carrying her bathrobe
and slippers, not having been able to get them
into her suitcase. My own traveling being on
the timid and panicky side—Henry calls it the
chambered-nautilus strain in me — I felt re-
proached by this splendid poise, though not for
long. Humility is not my forte, and whenever I
dwell for any length of time on my own shortcomings, they gradually begin to seem mild,
harmless, rather engaging little things, not at all
like the staring defects in other people's characters.

There was a long, long interval of waiting for
the customs man—though an English customs
official is almost worth waiting several hours
for, even on a dock called Pneumonia Alley. It
was noon before we got through. We took our
jeunes filles to lunch and plied them with bits of
practical advice, which were given and received

in that wild-spirited, irreverent, American manner which distresses the English so and seems to them the next worst thing in the world to telling how much you paid for things. The taboo on the word "stomach" struck the new arrivals as particularly delightful, and they wanted to know whether, in the event of indisposition in that region, they would have to ask for bicarbonate of soda by sign language or whether they would be permitted to say they had you-know-what-aches.

After lunch we put them on the London train, consigning them to a conductor to whom you would have trusted your favorite child and all your diamonds, and then we caught a train ourselves. I suppose it was hardly necessary to go all the way up there to meet them, for Englishmen are at their best on a dock or in a railroad station, and they would have been beautifully cared for. But if we had not gone and anything should have happened to them, we would have felt a little Herod-like.

June 16th

Henry's pockets are always eight months gone with old letters, and last night—after the most strenuous day he has had in months—he was suddenly moved to take time out and go through them. I noticed, after a while, that the process was being conducted on lines less leisurely and ruminative than usual, and it soon developed that somewhere between Exeter and Liverpool the inside topcoat pocket had been painlessly delivered of the wallet containing our passport and letter of credit. My mind leapt at once to the Home Office, English prisons and The Man Without a Country, but Henry, who has a kind of subterranean efficiency for all his untidiness, went without further words and telephoned all the places susceptible of being telephoned late in the evening. He telephoned again this morning, but though everybody he talked to displayed a positively knightly courtesy, so far nothing has turned up.

June 17th

The Exeter police called up this morning and said that the wallet had been found on the train by a baker's assistant and turned in to the police station at Weston-super-Mare. We decided to go and get it, instead of waiting for it to be sent down, as the town was not very far away and I was curious to see what a place called Weston-super-Mare would look like. It proved to be a seaside resort, commonplace and banal enough, but it had a police force whose hundred-horse-power, valve-in-head politeness made the constabulary a sort of unassuming salon. Big, gentle policemen who gave off quiet enjoyment of life in almost visible exhalations steered Henry

37

through the formalities, while I stood on one side and talked to a plain-clothes man about *Lorna Doone* and the Doone country in Devonshire. When the wallet had been restored, Henry arranged to leave some money for the man who had turned it in. This gratified the policemen immensely, and we all said good-bye in a welter of friendliness and Henry and I came away.

June 18th

I took Henry out to Yeobridge this morning, and he became pro-house as soon as we came down the narrow street, passed the old coaching inn (now translated into a pub) and caught sight of our prospective domicile sitting with a judicial air at the bend in the road. The house belongs to a small, elderly widow who has such an eighteenth-century clarity of outline that you would not dare leave a copy of Jane Austen around, for fear she should disappear into it. She has much more force than most of the Englishwomen I have met, these latter having had the strength drained out of them by the debilitating effort to be English Ladies. The poor things spend half their time gardening and the other half being respected and avoided by English men. They run off their dinners with a satin-smooth suavity which makes American hostesses look like victims of St. Vitus' dance, and they have brought their maids to such a state of ac-

38

quiescent obedience that they can ring the bell and, with the absolute certainty that it will be done, order Smithers to go down to the lily pond and feed herself to the carp. Nonetheless, their housekeeping (even to my uncritical eye) would be the better for a liberal dose of New World efficiency and the food . . . well, there is no use being repetitious. I have a theory about their hats. I think they keep them suspended on pulleys from the bedroom ceiling and when they want to put one on, they go and stand directly under it, pull a rope, and it drops down, smack, squarely on top of the head. Then, without touching a finger to it, they march out of the house.

But Mrs. Emmeline Turney, of Yeobridge, has survived the ordeal by refinement. Her house is burnished like a shield. When she showed me over it, she went masterfully up to the closets, opened them, and said in firm tones, "The hot water heater is *here*," instead of just waving vaguely in impossible directions and talking in murmurous fragments. Her clothes are not fashionable, but they have been chosen with care and she wears them as if she had the upper hand of them. She was dressed in grey today and her grey hair was pulled back from a somewhat coldly modeled face. She wears a black ribbon around her throat. Extensive travel and a good education of the nineteenth-century, complete-set-of-Dickens variety have made her anecdotal and well-informed in a pleasantly outmoded way. She does not begin her sentences with "You Americans . . ." She refers to Americans as "Your compatriots, my dear."

Mrs. Turney has a daughter who lives in Borneo and whom she is going to visit this winter, which is why Henry and I are able to rent her house. The daughter was sprinkled over our conversation like sugar over a doughnut—"Mydaughter's watercolors" . . . "Mydaughter's husband" . . . "Mydaughter's flair for languages" . . .

Henry is waiting—with a manner that looks like a sort of clever imitation of Slav fatalism— for me to turn out the light, but I am so full of the house at Yeobridge that it keeps me from being sleepy. We have taken the house, of course, and we have also taken the maid with it. Women in Exeter complain bitterly about the local talent in domestics, and certainly I am a living monument to the fact that they cannot cook. On the other hand, the maids I have seen have the pale, unlighted faces of the underpaid, and in this wilderness of Brussels sprouts and Ladies, who is there to teach them to cook?

The maid at Yeobridge, nevertheless, is a hand-tooled, presentation copy. She came to Mrs. Turney when she was fourteen, and was personally inducted by that dynamic matron

into the business of running a ménage. She is
now twenty. Her name is Phyllis and she has
blue eyes and red, red cheeks and she is so clean
she shimmers. When I was piloted into the
kitchen to look her over, she blushed like a well-
trained sunrise. Mrs. Turney speaks to her
kindly, but as from an immeasurable distance.

June 19th

We went out to Yeobridge this afternoon and
Mrs. Turney gave us tea, with Devonshire
cream, superlative strawberry jam and excellent sandwiches, compiled by a knowing hand.
Mrs. Turney's discussion of coal and the telephone and similar low, mercenary affairs was
so stately and impersonal that I felt as if we were
framing an international treaty, but she was exceedingly kind and made us very welcome. She
speaks to us both with a protective air, as if we
were very, very young and inexperienced, which
leaves us amused but also a little uncertain,
for we were prepared to be protective toward
her, as being very, very old and inexperienced.

The idea of going to Oxford next has been
hanging around in our minds for so long that it
has at length acquired the status of a definite
decision. Henry spent two terms at Oxford, ten
years ago. Actually, he says, it was a tepid inter-
lude. Though he was older than most of the
undergraduates, he had to eat in hall with the
first-year men, which made him feel like Father

Time. But it is a lovely place, he tells me, and I will like it.

We are all packed and ready to take the morning train to London tomorrow. It is an immense relief to have gotten the house at Yeobridge. Threatened with having to spend the winter in an unkempt modern villa or in one of those strongholds of dreariness which operate as hotels in Exeter, I was getting more and more uneasy. I began to think that, in coming here for a year, I had bitten off something which would be as much fun to chew as a bicycle tire. But now the prospect of traveling all summer has a reinforced attraction, since there is such an agreeable house to come back to in the autumn.

I have been here twelve days. Already, it seems to me, I have learned what to expect from Exeter, and what not to expect from it. Renaissance masonry, Tudor houses, old mahogany tables, and unlimited supplies of urbanity—Yes. Decent food, or any human relationship not virtually embalmed in good taste—No. What Yeobridge will turn out to be, I cannot tell. It looks like the kind of place where the conversation seldom gets above the Vicar's cough and never gets below it. But the house is ultrasatisfactory and for the present, that suffices. I feel as if I had come into focus.

PART II

Footloose

LONDON—There is commuter's blood in my veins and my mind throbs with racial memories of the Grand Central, so I was taken aback, when we came into London today, at the grimy ugliness of Waterloo Station. Henry tells me Waterloo is typical of the big London stations, but when we stepped from the train into a cavernous shed churning with smoke and howling with steam, I plucked at him and said, "Good God, they've brought us to the roundhouse!" Looked at more closely, though, the station has the same blend of shabbiness and imperturbable good nature which seems to characterize the English whenever they are not trying to be genteel. Incredible taxis flounce in and out—tall, antiquated machines as innocent of streamlining as a top hat and with such a small wheelbase that when they turn around they look double-jointed. The porters behave like slightly idealized versions of themselves and the trains . . . well, there is something definitely ingratiating about a train when it is so small you could get it into your pocket and have room left over for a flashlight.

London is straining at the seams with tourists and consequently we find ourselves in an old-fashioned hotel sacred to the clergy and the military and refined to a degree which makes the moderately impressionable visitor feel as if he had been included in an aspic. The bedrooms are lofty and twilit; the elevator moves as mournfully to its destination as Charon's ferry, with much less certainty of getting there; and in the long, dim corridors, an occasional fugitive gleam from a clerical collar provides the only sign of life. Brontosaurian furniture with a dark, primeval finish glooms from every possible corner and from the impossible ones as well. The service is slow, unsmiling and ponderous. About the whole enterprise there hovers an air of stately amateurishness, as if somebody's house had suddenly been turned into a hotel and the servants were resentful at having strangers around.

The hotel guests fit perfectly into the atmosphere and *décor*—having, most of them, a flinty cast of face which would hopelessly handicap a fo'c'sle worker, but which the unco guid can afford. The clergymen are the mildest feature of the landscape. They run to silver hair, and scan Henry and me wistfully over their copies of the *Church Times*. The clergymen's wives, on the other hand, are no more wistful than Gibraltar. Their hostility arises, I think, from my having automatically lit a cigarette in the dining room after dinner last night. Before I had even laid down the match, a Prime Min-

46

isterial man came thudding up, in the nearest thing to a hurry he could muster, and asked me not to smoke. By a perceptible effort, he stopped himself from adding, "There are ladies present." I doused the fatal instrument with lightning promptitude, but it was a good seven minutes before the last indignant handkerchief had folded its wings and gone back to its reticule and the last manufactured cough died protestingly away.

The military men do not regard us with hostility. They do not see us at all. Red-faced, white-moustached, trailed by dusty, timeless little wives who suggest immortelles, they are the kind of men whose friends describe them as bits of martinets. Their eyes look like affronted oysters and fill me with a well-nigh unquenchable desire to move a pencil slowly toward their noses and see if those glassy orbs will cross. Nevertheless, there is something peculiarly satisfying about the hotel guests. It is their symmetry, I suppose. They are so perfect of their kind. And I am grateful to them for the little quiver of amusement I get every time I realize how much their hard, sour, unripe maturity reminds me of greening apples.

June 22nd

The north transept of Westminster Abbey, by which you go in, is tall and shadowy, like a church, and has a churchly smell, but it is so stuffed with monuments and plaques that the traveler automatically begins to look around for price tags. What makes this petrified forest even more disappointing is that most of the people commemorated in it are not buried in the Abbey. A man's grave, since one necessarily thinks of death in terms of life, has authenticity, but a monument per se is a shabby sell-out—unless, of course, it happens to be a work of art. And a snowstorm of monuments like the collection in the Abbey could hardly be expected to touch or move anybody except a quarry enthusiast.

After a while, however, the statues and the busts thin out and the bona fide tombs begin. Good juicy tombs they are, too—Henry the Fifth, Charles the Second, Mary Queen of Scots, the Princes murdered in the Tower, Elizabeth and Bloody Mary sharing an ornate coffer—and I enjoyed them. To be sure, if I had any curiosity worthy of the name about English history, I would be in a library somewhere fattening up my slender knowledge of it, instead of careering fruitlessly from one Tudor effigy to another. But in the meantime (a meantime which, to be candid, is likely to be indefinitely prolonged), there is a very pleasant sense of achievement in discovering that Ben Jonson is under the floor, whereas Chaucer has been let into the wall.

The Chapel of Henry the Seventh is the best part of the Abbey. It is the first architecture I have seen that really does suggest frozen music. The walls and roof are almost solidly composed of ornament—statues and niches and grilles and carving—but the room is so high that it absorbs the decoration like a chord absorbing component notes. Severe in its proportions and exuberant in its details, it has the dissolving motion of music, and the woven intricacy and plaited multitudinousness. A spider web in stone, Washington Irving calls it (according to the guidebook). Being an aristocrat and an Anglophile, he did not, I suppose, like to comment on what a stroke of pure genius it was to put Henry the Seventh in the middle of it.

The Chapel and the royal tombs and all the Abbey back of the high altar were not open to the public except in conducted parties, which was how we saw them. There were about twenty people in our group, mothers with children, old ladies, self-conscious men in shabby clothes, and a few sailors. A black-gowned verger took us around. He strode along some ten yards ahead of us, his gown bellying in the breeze so that he looked from the rear as if he ought to tack. Periodically, he wheeled about and waited for us to come up, his hands tucked into his flowing sleeves, his face taut with the strained composure of a man who wishes to God he had a cigarette. When we got within speaking distance, he unfurled one sleeve in the direction of a tomb and said crisply, "Anne-of-Cleves-mind-the-step." We all crowded solemnly around Anne of Cleves, or whoever it happened to be, and tightened our faces into expressions of studious interest. The verger stood as far away from us as he could, without actually being out of sight, and played with a bunch of keys. At length one of the sailors backed tentatively away from the tomb, and we let our features slip into their normal aspect again and timidly moved towards our guide.

Here and there the verger stopped and made a speech. He talked without inflection, in flat, cheaply tailored sentences, and we stared at him from wide-open eyes and followed his gestures with our faces, like sunflowers. But he could not hurry us. We looked at everything he pointed out, and we kept on looking at it until somebody, bolder than the rest, gave us our cue to move away. Before the tour was half-way finished, the verger's toes were wiggling inside his shoes with impatience, and as he herded us into the cloisters, where he was supposed to leave us, his face was so distorted by the effort to get rid of us in a hurry and at the same time

Westminster Abbey

maintain an unbroken clerical calm, that he looked like a bad snapshot of himself.

After the conducted party broke up, Henry and I walked around by ourselves for a while and then went back to the hotel. Just before we left the Abbey, we saw the place in the nave where the Unknown Warrior is buried.

"The Sacred Cause Of Justice And The Freedom Of The World," I said, when we came out into the street. "I suppose they'll be taking it in at the waist and using it all over again, any minute now."

Henry shrugged.

"We'll have to call the next one the Unknowing Warrior," he said.

June 23rd

OXFORD—We took the bus from London to Oxford. Once the brassy-tasting edges of London are past, the country becomes an almost audibly fertile arrangement of hills and woods and park-like fields and cottages with explosively flowering gardens. But the approach to Oxford is flanked by rows of little workman's houses, corrosively unvaried, and the University, in the center of town, seems to be grimly trying to keep its head above the flung spray of a Morris car factory and similar lusty enterprises. The academic calm of the famous High Street approximates the studious tranquillity of

51

Times Square on election night. Back of the High Street façades of the colleges, however, there lies a more sheltered antiquity, an opium dream of lawns and leisure and old stone. It took me back to the days when I was the helpless thrall of a book called *The Little Lame Prince*, which was illustrated with just such casements and massive gateways and Gothic towers as these.

June 24th

Considering the strenuous industrial reality at its gates, I had expected to feel that the University, for all its haunting ripeness, was a plump and dropsical affair in comparison. But after peering up the damp stairways and into the dark, small-windowed rooms; after walking in the gardens and quadrangles sorting out old, carelessly collected knowledges of Oxford, one realizes that if the factory people outside the colleges live under the discipline of narrow means, the people inside live under almost every other kind of discipline except that of narrow means —from the fruity austerities of learning, through the iron rations of English gentlemanhood, down to the modest disadvantages of occupying cold stone buildings without central heating and having to cross two or three quadrangles to take a bath. When I said as much to Henry, he replied briefly that the University, like the Morris cars, is a patent process.

June 25th

From a purely tourist standpoint, Oxford is overpowering, being so replete with architecture and history and anecdote that the visitor's mind feels dribbling and helpless, as with an over-large mouthful of nougat. Yesterday afternoon we explored the colleges with one of the official guides, less from inclination on our part than from shameless insistence on his. He was a little old man in a dark-blue uniform, and under his tuition we went through the University like a strong draft. While he thrust us into paneled dining halls and shoved us in and out of Perpendicular chapels, he simultaneously hosed us down with information, some of which was startlingly inaccurate. I was just about to protest politely that John Wesley was not a "Premier of England" when the guide interrupted me by pointing to Merton College and saying that Robert Browning had been educated there.

"Oh, no," I burst out. "Browning was a nonconformist. He couldn't go to Oxford."

But the old man merely looked stubborn and answered doggedly that Robert Browning, the *poet* (vindictive glance at me), lived in them there rooms as you see plain enough in the corner.

After that I gave in, though when the old fellow got to Edward FitzGerald, Henry formed "Cambridge" with his lips. The guide did not notice.

"'E wrote," he began, still talking about FitzGerald, and hesitated. His face collapsed, and I thought he was going to cry. But instead he gave a cracked little chirp, lifted his head, and smiled a smile of pure bliss.

"'E wrote the Rubaiyat of Omer Komer."

June 26th

On the whole, I prefer the slapdash attentions of such a one as our old guide yesterday to the voluminous rectitude of the guidebook. The wrinkled ancient was spaciously misinformed and he contrived to turn the University into an obstacle race, but the guidebook—which I looked over this morning in the hope of picking up a few succulent associations—proved to be so spiky with information that reading it was like shaking hands with a clothesbrush. Nor do I warm to its diagrammatic, science-lecture prose. "Emerging into the High Street and turning to the left," the author begins drily, and I always expect him to end—"we are soon confronted by the vermiform appendix."

What saves the situation is that Henry, luckily, likes guidebooks. He has the common failing of his profession. He enjoys a statement twice as much if it appears in fine print, and anything that turns up in a footnote (as almost everything does in a guidebook) takes on the character of divine revelation. Thanks to this amiable weakness of his, the Cromwells and Lauds and Amy Robsarts and Sir Thomas Mores come to me all cleaned up and laid out neatly on platters, Henry having joyfully done the pioneer work of hacking them out of their matrix of negligible scientists, obscure poets, Saxon chronicles and Field Marshal Haig.

June 27th

STRATFORD—We left Oxford precipitately. Ten years of looking forward to Europe had more or less prepared me for the lovely, blended ancientry of the University, but I was taken off guard by the spongy weather, the draggled food we ate in Oxford restaurants, and the heartless brown wicker chairs in the hotel lounge. They were chairs of such a sterile shininess that they made my tongue shrink, as if I were tasting the varnish instead of just looking at it. Henry made no objection when I said I wanted to move on, though he remarked equably that we would certainly lose caste with all our academic acquaintance if, with the whole summer before us, we stayed a mere three days or so in Oxford.

"We won't tell," I said. "We'll say we stayed

two weeks, and only left when the Warden of All Souls cleaned us out in a crap game."

June 28th

Indefensible the flight from Oxford may have been, but it brought us into good weather. The countryside around Stratford is green and plenteous and full of repose. Cushioned with trees and padded with hedgerows, it runs up into little mattress slopes which fade imperceptibly away again. In the villages, the thatched houses rest on their gardens like cuff-links on jeweler's cotton. An aimless walk through this engaging landscape, on which we started out this morning, ended by taking the whole day. We turned down whatever paths looked promising; crossed empty, sunlit fields that were rough underfoot and hard going, for all their smooth-looking grass; and followed wavy lanes which perpetually unfurled new arrangements of trees and cows. Occasionally we passed farmhouses, sheltered with barns and looking like people who have the covers pulled up to their chins. At every farmhouse a big, blurry dog bounded out and gave us a twenty-one-gun salute. Henry flinched at the dogs.

"Look!" I said, with a genial wave of the hand. "His tail is wagging. He likes you."

"Oh, yes," assented Henry bitterly. "He wants to be my Valentine."

56

Around eleven o'clock in the forenoon, we got completely lost in an expanse of fields and sat down under a big pine tree to rest. Henry, in spite of the dogs, had developed an enthusiastic Hardy Pioneer mood in the course of the morning, and he applied himself vigorously to the map. But apparently we had either walked right off it or had never been on it at all. In the end a toothless farmer came along and told us that we could not get lunch any nearer than the village of Loxley. He obligingly gave us directions how to get there, though when Henry offered him the map for demonstration purposes, he waved it away.

"Aw, vhem vhings . . ." he said, with whimsical contempt.

At Loxley a surprised but compliant lady who had TEAS lettered tentatively on her gate, gave us lunch. Her house was dazzlingly ugly, but clean, and we closed in gratefully on the cold ham and new-laid eggs and lettuce from the garden. I congratulated her on the view from her doorstep—the house stood on rising ground and overlooked a wide sweep of fields and copses.

"I'm from Birmingham," she said. She might have been an expatriate angel explaining that he was from the right hand of God. "It's very quiet here."

"But such a lovely place to live . . .," I began.

"Yes," she answered with finality, and I rec-

57

ognized the antiseptic voice of a woman who has been argued to a standstill and has fallen back on passive resistance.

The TEAS lady told us the name of a village where we could get a bus back to Stratford, so we embarked in that direction. I was walking ahead. Nature, when she fashioned Henry and me, never intended us to walk together. If I had to stump around on a mermaid's tail, I would still be an inevitable twenty yards ahead of him. I climbed thoughtlessly up a gate and only realized as I slithered down the other side that willy-nilly I was keeping a tryst with a bull. The bull looked at me and stopped chewing. I once read somewhere that when a human being is afraid, his glands give off a chemical which animals can smell, so that they know he is frightened. Through a seething fog of panic, I remembered this and knew dimly that it must be an old wives' tale, or the bull would have gotten a blast from me sufficient to waft him into the next county.

Henry came up to the gate and climbed over. The bull breathed out with a long whoofing sound. Henry collected my wrist and walked unconcernedly on, pulling me after him. I had to be pulled. My knees could have been stirred with a spoon. The bull turned his head to look after us, but did not move. When we got safely into the next field, I asked Henry how he could turn pale at a harmless little farm dog, and yet walk composedly past fifteen hundred pounds of professional aggressiveness.

"Matter of dignity," he said. "Rather be gored any day than have my pants chewed off."

June 29th

We are staying at one of the "Bed and Breakfast" houses which are the equivalent of the American "Tourist" places, except that they are a very little cheaper and a great deal less attractive. Ours, which looks fairly typical, is a small, cramped establishment wedged uncomfortably into a row of other small, cramped establishments. A steely and suspicious matron presides over it. She has a mouth which ought to be left out in the woods to catch bears. Our room, extravagantly small, is decorated to the eyebrows in a suffocating shade of pink. Though a rusted, saturnine bathroom opens off the head of the tiny staircase, guests are expected to wash in the bedrooms. For this purpose Henry and I have been supplied with an acid-green bowl and pitcher which have evidently known each other carnally, for they are surrounded by various acid-green pledges of affection—a pin tray, a hair receptacle, a toothbrush mug, and several other little toddlers of no discernible function.

A sudden access of financial prudence inspired the choice of this bower. I need a coat

and Henry has grown frayed as a chrysanthe-
mum, so we are going to have some new clothes
made when we get back to London. There is a
tailor in Savile Row who has made suits for
Henry before, and even old and grey and full of
sleep, as they are now, they have a faint, incor-
rigible distinction. New, they must have been
downright poetic. In the meantime, however,
we institute compensating economies. The
straitened regime is harder on me than on
Henry, who never knows whether he is comfortable or not until it is pointed out to him. I,
unhappily, am a natural-born voluptuary. I do
not mind taking sectional baths with two pints
of water in the country, where it seems unexcep-
tional and goes along with fresh air, old clothes
and being sleepy by nine o'clock in the evening.
But segmented bathing in this weary, con-
stricted, suburban household has nothing of
rural simplicity about it, only skimpiness and
inadequacy, and it makes you feel when you
finish like a postage stamp that has been licked
and then not used.

June 30th

The Shakespeare Memorial Theater, where
we went last night to see *Lear*, is a red-brick,
poker-face, modernistic building which would
do very well anywhere else, but which is violently inappropriate in a village as devoutly

Elizabethan as Stratford. To turn the corner and come unexpectedly upon it, rearing up from the pastoral landscape, produces the same effect as looking idly round in church and seeing somebody smoking. Henry asked me this morning if I did not think *Lear* reads better than it acts. I had perforce to admit, not having seen it before, that I was sunk in cloddish sleep throughout most of the performance. I had had a strenuous day, and the theater seats are like downy, fledgling bathtubs. My only clear recollection is of the man in the seat next to me saying confidently, as the first act curtain went up, "Now this is going to be about Tamburlaine."

Later

Henry is out doing errands, and I am taking advantage of his absence to write a few more notes. This room is so small it could be wrapped up and sent through the mail and when we are both in it together, we have scarcely space to stir a finger. An odor of cabbage, entwined with coal gas, works its way tactlessly up the stairs. But visions of sugar plums sustain me, for at the end of the long prelude of Bed and Breakfasting is the house at Yeobridge, standing by itself and facing the open country, redolent, in the manner of country houses, with straw and must and wood fires and furniture polish.

The English of the gentlemanly persuasion

(my little sample of them, that is) seem to me only remotely human, but their houses look far more human than comparative American homes. American interiors tend to have no happy medium between execrable taste and what is called "good taste" and is worn like a wart. But the English have a series of advantages over us in this respect. For one thing, they have a knack of inheriting beautiful highboys and tables and desks and side boards, and as these objects come to them easily, they use them easily. For another, they are not influenced in their house-furnishing by shiny pictures in magazines. In England, magazines do not have the green-bay-tree aspect that they do in America, and no English advertising, in any medium, is likely to put ideas into anybody's head. When you furnish a house in England, you have to rely on your own judgement—supplemented, not infrequently, by your great-great-grandmother's chests of drawers. Furthermore, twenty years in the same house is regarded as a mere pausing in transit, which eliminates the Procrustean awkwardnesses common to the dwellings of rolling stones. I thought that the rooms we saw when we were dining and house-hunting in Exeter were, in general, full of distinction and individuality. They made the Schrafft-like interiors at home seem, looking back on them, floridly imitative.

England in a burst of generosity endowing us with more good weather this morning, we went off on another walk. I had thought a second excursion might be anticlimactic, but it turned out to be blood brother to the last one. Under the heat of the sun, my mind melted and ran down into my skin and muscles, where it felt much better than it does in its natural habitat. We lunched at a TEAS place again, on stale cheese and oily canned tongue, but ate in the garden this time and had strawberries and cream for dessert. English strawberries call for more superlatives than a single person can easily lay his hands on. Nearly twice as big as ours, they have a quintessential strawberriness about them compared to which the American variety are strawberries of ectoplasm.

Today's TEAS lady was a mild-mannered housewife with a pleasant, one-piece personality which made us inclined to call her talkative rather than garrulous. She is a native of the village where she lives and while we ate, entertained us with a Homeric narrative of the village May Day festival. Her own children being all grown up, she had had her eye on a delicate, blonde little girl as May Queen timber and was keenly disappointed when the choice fell to an exuberant brunette. Henry and I joined in her placid triumph that the vigorous brunette defaulted through chicken pox and the anemic but scatheless blonde was inducted anyway. After we left, Henry complimented me on how well I am learning to talk to strangers.

"I don't know," I replied doubtfully, recalling the fluency of the TEAS lady. "Perhaps it's just that the strangers are learning to talk to me."

I have just been writing a note to Mrs. Turney. Mrs. Turney's flair for inheritance is conspicuous, even in England. She has tea on taper Sheraton from her own family and dines with a battery of Hepplewhite from her husband's. Upstairs in the bedrooms ladder-back Chippendale chairs flank chests of drawers whose patina is palpable as a smile. The house at Yeobridge, however, is too much a woman's house for impeccable repose. Though the bedrooms have been kept relatively uncomplicated, the downstairs rooms are scuppers awash with knickknacks—bowls, vases, trays, paperweights, fancy pencils, prayer books, clocks, china figures, dance programs, fans, candlesticks, ivory chessmen and babies' shoes. "The ornaments," Mrs. Turney calls them. Some of them are noteworthy in their own right, and some are obviously cherished because of associations with Mydaughter, but they are all so indiscriminately crowded together that the general effect is pure flotsam and jetsam. When we move in, in the fall, I shall put most of them away, if it can be done without unduly alarming the handmaiden Phyllis.

July 2nd

Anne Hathaway's cottage and Mary Arden's cottage are sufficiently beautiful, with their brilliant gardens, to soften the most obdurate foe of quaintness. But like all the other high spots in Stratford, they have been provided with postcard stands and with neat custodians whose easy, mechanical Poet-worship had me looking sharply to see if they were plugged into the wall. All of Stratford, in fact, suggests powdered history—add hot water and stir and you have a delicious, nourishing Shakespeare. The inhabitants of the town occupy themselves with painting SWEET ARE THE USES OF ADVERSITY around the rims of moustache cups for the tourist trade; the wide, cement-paved main street is fringed with literary hot dog stands; and in the narrow lanes adjoining, wrinkled little beldames of Tudor houses wearily serve out their time as tea rooms.

It costs a shilling to cross any doorstep in Stratford, and once inside, the visitor finds himself on the very spot where Shakespeare signed his will or wrote *The Tempest* or did something or other which makes it necessary to charge an additional sixpence for the extra sanctity involved. Through all the shrines surge English and American tourists, either people who have read too much Shakespeare at the expense of good, healthy detective stories or people who have never read him at all and hope to get the same results by bumping their heads on low beams. Both categories try heroically to appear deeply moved, an effort which gives their faces a draped look. Were it not for the countryside round about, I would not stay an hour in Stratford—I keep expecting that somebody all dressed up as the immortal bard will come rushing out with a jingle of bells and a jovial shout, and I will have to confess apologetically that I am a big girl now and too old to believe in Shakespeare.

Later

We have an American schoolteacher staying at Bed and Breakfast with us. She is a small, dynamic woman whose manner suggests very clearly that life had better watch its step, or she will take down its little pants and spank, but she has been kind enough to warn us that if we are going to Norway and Sweden, we had better lose no time in making boat reservations, as the cabins are usually all taken up for weeks in advance.

66

CAMBRIDGE—I like Cambridge better than Oxford. It is less sonorously antique than the other University, but it has a more livable, reassuring kind of beauty. Oxford wears its battered Gothic like a halo. Cambridge is earthier in sagely smiling brick. The Plum-Colored Court of St. John's, the Great Gate of Trinity, the snug corner of Queens' where Erasmus is said to have lived, the soundless seclusion of the Fellows' Garden at Magdalene, go into the mind as cosily as ink going into a blotter.

And then there is the stretch of smooth and shiny little river, with colleges standing along it like matron divinities, familiar but effulgent, and watching their gardens run down to the water. It is a matchless compilation of trees and stream and architecture and it is called, restrainedly, the Backs. There have been only a few hours of sunshine since we came here, but loitering along the Backs, even under an unprepossessing sky, is a form of lotus-eating. The bridges worm their way through clouds of weeping willow, Queens' College rises sheer out of the water and has an apoplectically blossoming garden next to it, the irresolute current fingers at the weeds, and in the background the spires of King's College Chapel lift delicately over broad lawns. It has the velvet unbelievableness of an incipient swoon.

The beauty of Cambridge seems to be nuclear and kernelish; beyond the colleges and the heart of the town are flat, feeble suburbs, golf courses and wrappers from chocolate bars. On the strength of Rupert Brooke's poem, we walked out to Grantchester today. Henry bought a copy of Rupert Brooke so that I could read the poem, which I did not know. There are some lines that I like very much, but they are interpolated between big gobbets of whimsy which appear to have been imported into the poem from a gymnasium. The Grantchester excursion was sketchy. Just before lunch a heavy shower came on and we spent most of our time there standing hopelessly under a tree. When the shower was over, we applied for lunch to a large house which advertised Garden Teas. Garden meals, in fact, were the only kind it had. Two merciless old ladies conducted the enterprise, and rain or no rain, they refused to let us into the house. We had lunch on a soaked bench in a swimming orchard and held our hats over the plates to keep off the drippings from the trees.

No one in this country, not the people we met in Exeter or the porters, landladies, salesgirls and bus conductors we have seen since, ever appears to be in a hurry. Time, the English believe, drops like manna from heaven, and there is plenty more where that came from. Henry and I have fallen fathoms deep into this attitude and are idling self-indulgently about Cambridge, reading and walking in the college gardens, when we ought to be in London arranging for the Scandinavian trip.

I have been worrying a little about Phyllis. To be born and raised in a Devonshire village and then spend six impressionable years under the active influence of Mrs. Emmeline Turney hardly constitutes an ideal preparation for living with a couple of smart-alec New Yorkers. I suppose she will have to fall back on reflecting that at least we are not in trade. Henry suggests, however, that she probably goes into Exeter twice a week to an American movie and is no doubt waiting hopefully for us to wear silver fox on our night clothes and shoot from the hip.

July 6th

Henry pointed out this morning that we ought to be ripe for another cathedral, not having seen one in some time, so after lunch we took the bus from Cambridge to Ely. Compared with Exeter Cathedral, which is small and demure, the one at Ely is a big, rangy athlete of a sanctuary. I had had a preconceived notion that cathedrals are always grey, but the exterior of Ely is the color of the old brownstone fronts in New York seen through smoked glasses. The inside, however, has retained a pleasing pallor and an even more gratifying simplicity. No statues or even chairs flaw the long vista of the nave. There are only Norman columns of primal plainness and vasty altitude, and between them pure space and rich, subaqueous light dissolving down from towering shafts of windows.

When we had looked with attention at the monks' door, the Galilee porch and a shattered seventh-century cross, and had strolled receptively past the ancient, solid buildings adjoining the Cathedral, we climbed the western tower. The view from the top is a bright-colored, comfortable synthesis of farms, red roofs, neat bunches of trees, and mile on mile of flat, fat, smacking green fields laced with sober hedgerows. Ascending the tower was strenuous; coming down was terrifying. The staircase is dark as a grave and much more complicated, being a spiral in which most of the steps have been worn away to shapeless mounds. By the time we reached the bottom again, my legs were trembling like captured things and were just about as cooperative.

We had tea at a hotel near the Cathedral—a pleasant place, with flowered wallpaper, a grandfather clock and a large infusion of brass

candlesticks. Plush chairs and Victorian ornaments scattered liberally about made it look
overstuffed, but saved it from the smirk of conscious quaintness. Two Englishwomen of about
thirty were ordering tea as we came in. Tall,
currycombed, fashionable creatures they were,
and the bodiless staccato of their well-bred English voices was like the sound of typewriters borne
on the wind. They had been alone in the salon,
and regarded our entrance as a species of rape;
but after Henry helped them to move a heavy
chair nearer the fireplace, their manner softened
down into surprise and approbation, as if Henry
were a small boy who had said something amaz-
ingly intelligent.

To me they were an epochal event, being the
first Englishwomen I have seen who wore good
clothes and wore them with distinction. I should
judge, from my observation so far, that there
must be thousands of British females every year
who are absent-mindedly collected by the laun-
dryman. Their universal ineptitude about
clothes fills me with a great pity and an overwhelming desire to take them in hand. But I
know in advance it would be fruitless. The trouble goes deeper than their having no eye for line
and no feeling for color, though they are as dew-
ily unaware of line and color as an orangoutang.
The fundamental difficulty is that they are
ashamed of having legs and waists and breasts,

71

and so they muffle themselves up as if their bodies were something that had to be smuggled through the customs. I suppose the English reply to this criticism is that American women spend too much time and energy on their clothes, which I think is true. But what do Englishwomen spend their time and energy on instead? I ask it, who have eaten their cooking.

July 7th

The days obligingly mould themselves into a generous routine. In the mornings Henry makes notes against his lectures for the fall and I write letters. I enjoy writing letters; in my self-supporting days I was a stenographer, and it still feels to me like slipping a leash to write to somebody and sign my own name at the bottom. The afternoons we spend picking over the colleges and in the evenings we read. The current Bed and Breakfast house is a vast improvement on the one at Stratford. It is occupied by undergraduates in the winter and affords us a sitting room of our own as well as a bedroom. The landlady, who limps, gives us fried tomatoes every morning for breakfast even when we ask her not to, but her disposition has the brimming passivity of a millpond and spills out into a smile which uses up all the flesh and wrinkles of her face.

I am face to face with the possibility that I have hay fever. My childhood was spent in all sorts of entangling alliances with ragweed and goldenrod, and if I sneezed, it kept the family in table talk for two weeks. But ever since the long walks we took in Stratford, I have suffered a sea change. My eyes itch in long crescendos, my nose tickles to madness, and my handker-chiefs are developing fins. Henry suggests a doc-tor, but I have a theory that germs and infirmi-ties like to play the grandstand, and that if one can manage to ignore them, they will go sheep-ishly away. Besides, should it really be hay fever, there is very little a doctor can do at this late stage. What I need is a harbor master. Oh, well. I pin my hopes to its subsiding when I leave the gardens of Cambridge and get to the relative barrenness of London.

July 9th—Remnant Counter

I

I have been in England just over a month, and the shops and buildings and trains and automobiles have come to look entirely natural, instead of small and strange. Sometimes the tininess of everything, and the way in which every available inch of ground is under cultiva-tion, make me feel a little smothered and produce a transient hankering for ragged waysides, careless miles of woods, and Size 40 in a sky. But the England I have seen is lovely to look upon beyond anything I had imagined before I came—though, to be sure, the only time I am ever aware of having any imagination is in cases of anticipated calamity—and I am glad to be going to live in the midst of it for a while.

II

Aside from the Warden of the hostel in which we stayed, and she *was* insular, Henry and I met with impeccable hospitality and a really genial welcome in Exeter. Nevertheless, we occasionally (though, to be just, not often) heard a silky intonation suggesting that it must be a great treat for us barbarian *Ausländer* to come and have a look at a civilized country. When a person says a thing is civilized, he often means nothing more than that he is used to it. One of the things I am used to is reading lamps, but the English idea of lighting seems to be a single shaded bulb hanging from the middle of the ceiling, so that people who want to do close work have to cluster like flies on a grease spot in the one small area of illumination. Even the silky-intonation-ers ought to be satisfied with my respect for England during the daytime, but when night falls I tell myself with a tolerant smile that after all,

I am here on a vacation and I don't mind roughing it a bit.

III

It would never occur to the English to coin a phrase like "service with a smile." They cannot imagine any other kind. But though the country reeks with graceful good-nature, the smile is often rather better than the service. A traveler in England has to fight his way through crowds of sunny menials who are everlastingly whisking his shoes off and carting them away to be polished. When the shoes come back, however, they are not polished at all, only smeared amateurishly with paste. Since I have been in England, it has come home to me like a bullet how incorrigibly American I am. It has come home like another bullet that, taken all in all, I am glad of it. I admire profoundly the English sense of leisure and indifference to the passing of time, but one can hardly help seeing that the reason the English have more time is because they do things less thoroughly. They always stop before they have finished the job.

A good many jobs, I suppose, stand in no essential need of finishing. It is not a law of nature that shoes should be shiny or that, provided it works properly, a toilet should refrain from looking as if it had been whittled out of the village stocks. And yet it seems to me the English

75

pay dearly for their repose in slovenliness, discomfort and incuriosity. My fantastic countrymen work themselves into tatters trying to establish havens of hundred-percentness in a universe geared to incompletion. The English, taking the opposite tack, eschew the temptations of achievement and symmetry and lie quietly down to let the universe roll over them. It frees the juices, I am bound to admit, but it leaves the poor Britons considerably mashed.

July 12th

We came to London two days ago and have been active, ever since, as grubs when a stone is turned over. A black coat is under way for me in Savile Row and a grey-blue suit for Henry. Savile Row acts as if it thought it were the Acropolis, but Henry says wait and see. Henry is having one of the streaks of silent, deadly efficiency which periodically emerge from the evening mist of his character. Shopping, letters, inquiries, arrangements and telephone calls are being cleaned up right and left—and with far more speed and incisiveness than I could bring to them, whose competence in that direction, though more constant, is more diluted. In the course of his arrowy phase, Henry has been to a travel agent to ask about Scandinavia. The agent suggests a trip which has our fingers itching for suitcase handles, but confirms the Amer-

The English eschew the temptations of achievement

ican schoolteacher at Stratford and makes no
promises about train, boat and hotel reservations. He is going to let us know, which sounds
as dubious as it does when you are applying for
a job.

July 13th

London has regrettably done nothing at all
for my hay fever, but being here is a pleasant
change. Henry has been dusting off his London
acquaintance and after the idle dabbling in the
provinces, this brisker and less two-against-the-
worldly kind of life has tang. It feels more . . .
well, more American. I suppose I did not come
to England to feel American, but it seems to be
very hard to feel English.

July 15th

A publisher who was in Oxford with Henry
asked us to a party he was giving last night, so
we had our evening clothes pressed and set off
feeling rather gay and anticipatory. It was not
a mood, however, destined to last very long.
Our host greeted us affably and told us where
to leave our wraps. When we came back from
leaving them, he escorted us to the doorway of
a large room and then, just as I was ponderously
framing a sentence about how kind it had been
of him to invite us, he vanished. He just wasn't

77

there any more. I blinked, and Henry said, "Remind me to ask him how he does that."

Left to our own devices, we decided the best thing to do was to assume an aspect of composure and make a little voyage of exploration. There were three large rooms, tall and handsome and furnished in the gravely comfortable, tempered-eighteenth-century manner at which the English are peculiarly adept. The rooms were filled with well-fed, well-washed, well-groomed men and with a quantity of women rather better dressed than the matrons of Exeter, but still looking as if they had all changed clothes with each other, just for a lark. As was to be expected, there was not, in the whole company, a single person we knew.

We finished our tour and stood in a corner of one of the rooms, feeling sad and disillusioned and as superfluous as lovers' knots on a locomotive. People were distributed around in little clusters and in big clusters, all talking gaily and all apparently very well known to each other. Our host was nowhere in sight.

"What do we do now?" I asked.

Henry smiled sorrowfully.

"Have you anything white," he said, "that we could run up on a pole?"

One of the other guests came towards us carrying, rather unskillfully, three drinks. I involuntarily smiled a little, for the drinks were spill-

ing over on to his wrist and, judging from the
expression on his face, running up his sleeve.
But when he glanced up and saw me smiling, he
gave me a look of pitying disapproval which
would have been more appropriate had I been
soliciting him on the street, and went gravely on
his way.

I looked around again at those cohesive
groups of men and women. It occurred to me
that perhaps we were supposed to take the in-
itiative and go up and talk to people. But nobody seemed to be roaming around at large, and
forcing a way into one of those tight little clusters appeared about as practicable as approaching the Archbishop of Canterbury and asking
him if he were doing anything tonight.

Man-hunts, when I read about them in the
paper, always distress me acutely on behalf of
the poor fugitive, but the ensuing two hours
made me think that possibly his position is not
altogether unenviable. We sat on a sofa and had
a cigarette. A man came past and stepped on
my foot and said, "I beg your pardon." We
went and stood in front of a fireplace. Another
man, tall and middle-aged and with a kindly
face, approached us and asked diffidently if we
were the Americans. Just as Henry opened his
mouth to reply, a woman screamed, "Hilary,
darling!" in a voice like the upper registers of a

wind machine and the middle-aged man excused himself and went away.

We sat on the sofa and smoked. We stood in front of the fireplace and smoked. We walked through all the rooms again. Then Henry pointed out that as there were drinks in evidence, there must be some place to get them. After a little reconnoitering, we discovered a small room off on one side, empty except for a man with a white coat and a face like the outside of a refrigerator. He silently gave us champagne cocktails, which we as silently drank. Then he silently gave us another cocktail, which we also drank in silence, and then we went back to the fireplace.

It began to seem to me that people were looking at us curiously. We walked through all the rooms a third time and coming upon a bookcase, inspected some of the titles. They were mostly about birds and gardening. "If we had the guts of an ant," I said to Henry, indicating the books, "we'd find some conspicuous chairs and curl up with a couple of those." Instead, we returned to the sofa.

Suddenly we noticed our host approaching us. I was glad to see him in the flesh and to realize that he had not, after all, been yanked off by imperative wraiths who had decided to add a note of class and tone and Oxford breeding to the spirit world. But my heart sank when I saw from his unslackened pace that he was merely on his way to somewhere else. He asked us urgently if we had found out where the drinks were, but was out of earshot before there was time to answer.

We sank back on the sofa. I tied knots in my handkerchief and then carefully untied them and Henry turned a package of matches over and over in his fingers.

"Let's play Beaver," I said.

"Can't," replied Henry gloomily. "Nothing but moustaches."

I relapsed into silence again. "I'll give somebody," I decided to myself, "fourteen more knots to come up and speak to us." So I tied fourteen more knots, taking care not to hurry, and then I tied two more, just for good measure. After that, I stood up.

"I'm going," I said equably.

Henry stood up too.

"Might as well," he answered, after a moment's thought. "First thing you know somebody will penetrate our incognito."

We found our coats again and met in the hall. This time the other guests really did look at us curiously. Henry murmured something about saying good-bye to the host.

"You can't," I said, pulling my wrap around me. "He changed himself into a Tom Collins and somebody drank him." But Henry waylaid a man who was crossing the hallway and gave him, to his great surprise, an anemic little excuse to be relayed to the publisher. Then we let ourselves out.

July 16th

All our money for the year is in a letter of credit which seems to have been designed by the same man who was responsible for the snows of yesteryear. Nor will the trip to Norway and Sweden be precisely a restorative. We will go, if it is possible to get there, but sometimes gloomy apprehensions prey upon us of being reduced to living on the dust from pencil sharpeners before the twelvemonth is out.

For reasons of economy, therefore, we came to London virtuously resolved to continue avoiding hotels and fortified with a list of furnished rooms culled by Henry from the *Times*. The first two places we looked at were haggard old houses with antimacassars, Robinson Crusoe plumbing, and the darkly greasy look which comes from years of wear and tear and which no amount of cleaning can obviate. But the third house was a tall old family residence near the Marble Arch—a simple, pleasing structure only recently converted into what the manager calls a private hotel. The green front door is newly painted, the hallway winks with the pristine whiteness of the staircase, and the rooms themselves are fresh and clean and brilliantly unused. There are closets in place of the customary stunted wardrobe in which shoes mingle inadvisedly with coat-tails, and the hot water rushes out in a thick, noisy stream, instead of threading its way down so coyly that you turn it on in the morning in order to have enough to wash your hands at night. Furthermore, all this virginity is inexpensive.

The serpent enters Paradise in the person of the manager, a small, thin person with an artificially confiding manner and one shoulder unnaturally hunched up. "Just call me Captain Featherstone," he said warmly, as if he were a brigadier general who had demoted himself in the interests of cosiness. His cheeks are a morbid, unhealthy red, and he has a large and badly fitting glass eye with which he looks at you when he talks. After a while you realize he is not looking at you with the good eye. Having showed us the room, the Captain discoursed in his incurably intimate way on a number of people with titles who were represented as pawing ravenously at the door, waiting for a chance to stay in this house. So securely was the manager convinced of the fatal American weakness for titles, that he never even looked (with his good eye) to see how we were responding to these seductive tidbits. Henry's face would have imparted audience sense to a Juggernaut, but the Captain missed it completely and pursued his elegant baiting of the hook while the fish sat back and smirked knowingly at each other.

We took the room, not on account of the manager's rank allure, but because it seemed probable that we would not have to see very much of him. The first evening of our stay, he sent the chambermaid up to ask for a week's money in advance. Henry sent her back for the Captain. He could not understand, he said, when the maid had closed the door, why the manager had not mentioned payment in advance before we moved in; he did not like the look of the chambermaid's being sent up for the money; he thought there was something queer and irregular about the Captain; and he wanted to leave immediately. But the Captain was a long time in coming, and in the interval I persuaded Henry to stay. I was tired, and Henry's effectiveness and dispatch, at their most zenithy, do not extend to packing and unpacking. That was a week ago, and since then there have been only fleeting glimpses of the manager going up and down stairs on "lissom, clerical, printless toe." The breakfasts, it must be admitted, are evidently prepared in the evening and fanned all night, but nothing more untoward has happened than lukewarm tea and cold toast.

Captain Featherstone, *in propria persona*, asked for a week's money in advance again this morning. Henry paid, though he looked dubious about it. Much as I shrink from the prospect of removing to some atrabilious establishment like the others we looked at, I must admit that the manager's nods and becks and wreathèd smiles make you feel as if you were being iced, like a cake.

The little boy who shines the shoes brought us our breakfast this morning and, so far as we could tell, appeared to be running the whole house single-handed. We heard him in the hall bringing other breakfasts, and when Henry called downstairs to ask for the time, he was on the switchboard. After breakfast, as we went downstairs on our way out, we found the hall full of people. In one corner the chambermaids were backed against the wall, wide-eyed and silent, fingering their aprons. Eight or ten people, apparently lodgers, had formed a circle around two men, one of whom introduced himself—not without pride—as Mr. James, the owner. In the next breath he told us that Captain Featherstone had absconded last night, taking with him the housekeeping funds and the rents he had just collected from the tenants. The other man standing in the circle was a detective from the Metropolitan Police.

Mr. James is tall and well-dressed, with receding hair and a face like a freshly made bed, blank and white and slightly puffy. As victim, he was the local cynosure and the fumy attention had visibly gone to his head. The detective was calmer. He is stocky and dark-haired and would be handsome if he did not look so reliable. His speech has a trace of provincial accent, and his "sir" is almost "zur." While Mr. James gobbled up the fresh bit of audience represented by Henry and me, the detective stood by indulgently. Then he asked Henry how much money he had given to the Captain and on what days, slipped his notebook into his pocket, and with a manner at once shy and relentless disengaged himself from the conversational embrace of Mr. James. Beckoning pleasantly to the chambermaids, he disappeared down the kitchen stair.

That seemed to dispose of the affair for the time being, but Mr. James' excited self-importance had acquired runaway impetus and the lodgers were prancing with righteousness. We stood and listened to them for a few minutes. What was startling about their babbling, reckless comment was not so much the lack of charity, though that quality was entirely absent, as the lack of curiosity. It did not occur to a single person to wonder why the Captain was a thief, or what his background was (he speaks like an educated man), or how he got his crooked shoulder and his glass eye. With Saturnalian enthusiasm, the lodgers reiterated that he was a "wrong un" and an "outsider." They polished him off with spit, as children do apples, and under their hands the Captain, an ordinary windfall felon, began to look like a shiny, hand-picked monster. A slight awkwardness arose from Mr. James' declaring that he had trusted the Captain completely, whereas among the lodgers it was more fashionable to have suspected him from the first. But the owner, seeing how matters stood, slipped unobtrusively over to the Premonitionists and when Henry and I left, the company was flagellating lawbreakers in sweetest uniformity.

July 19th

We have a new manager, a redheaded and taciturn little Scotsman who—either out of sheer good sense or the national instinct for retrenchment or both—has cut down on the number of blower-offers. The blower-offers are the twelve people who stand on either side of the kitchen door in any English hotel and blow on all the food as it goes out, just in case there should be any traitorous vestige of heat in it. Judging from the delightful and altogether unexpected warmth of the breakfast this morning, the Scotsman is trying to get along with only one or two—and, as Henry said, eyeing the steam from the hot water pitcher, probably children at that.

Mr. James spends all his time at the hall table, ostensibly sorting mail. Tonight, when we came in, there were only two letters and the owner had worn them almost to shreds. I wanted to ask him whether he had no old ones he could use.

I am still racked with hay fever. Time was when I used rather to enjoy a good sneeze, but that was before I went in for mass production. Henry has gotten the name of a doctor from a man who owns a Bloomsbury book store which he, Henry, likes to poke about in and tomorrow I am going to make an appointment.

July 20th

The Divine Providence which sent us to the publisher's party is now trying to worm its way back into our good graces by letting us go to Scandinavia. The travel agent has produced, with an enormous triumphal flourish which we applauded proportionately, tickets to sail to Gothenburg, in Sweden, the third of next month and to return from Bergen, in Norway, on the twenty-sixth. In between, we are to have a week in Stockholm, followed by a week or so in Norway traveling by rail and fjord steamer and horse and carriage to a series of places which only sound the more exciting for having names which cannot possibly be pronounced without first drinking a glass of very, very bad sherry.

Normalcy Note

Mr. James has apparently gone back to whatever pursuits occupied him before the Featherstone coup, for the hall is empty today and the mail sleeps sweetly on the hall table.

July 21st

I went to the doctor yesterday, to see about my hay fever, mechanically and without much hope of relief, an attitude which the worthy practitioner did little to change. His office, up two flights of stairs in a decayed region near Golden Square, is full of large, broody furnishings which make the rooms navigable only by persons of a very light draft. The doctor himself is gaunt as a totem pole. He wore an antiquated black suit, the lapels of which had been dragged together in a reluctant rendezvous just over his collarbone. When I rehearsed my ailment, he listened with an attention which seemed too mournful and elaborate for a trifling tale of catarrh. I felt ashamed not to have a life-size, three-dimensional illness to offer him, something with a fair prospect of taking me off. After I had finished my apologetic plaint, he looked sadly up my nose and said in a stifled voice that there was nothing to be done for hay fever, if it were hay fever, but that I might try smelling salts.

"Well," I reflected, as I went down the stairs, "at least he didn't want to bleed me," so I worked my way out into Piccadilly Circus, where I found a drug store. I had had no experience of smelling salts, and coming from the shop into the street again, I uncorked the bottle, held it firmly under my nose, and drew a breath so deep as almost to suck in several little boys who were standing nearby. I do not know how I got home. The world was under water, ammonia water. A taxi wavered through the deeps and I have an impression I took it. When I could look about me once more, I saw that I had come home.

But the most outlandish part of the whole fantastic medication was that it wrought a cure. I suddenly noticed, while retailing the catastrophe to Henry, that fresh air was going boldly in and out of my nostrils as if it had the freedom of the city. Gingerly, with millimetric caution, I returned to the salts bottle. By last night I was so perceptibly less rheumy that I think if I had sent out a dove, it would have come back with an olive leaf in its mouth, and this morning, except for an occasional reminiscent sniff, I was cured.

Captain Featherstone has been caught. Our detective located and captured him in a small village in Kent, eight miles from the nearest railroad. I promptly queried the detective on how he had managed to trace the Captain, but he only laughed cheerily and replied, "Oh, we have our ways. . . ." The Captain is to be tried in a magistrate's court in about a week and I heard with relief, which was probably flabby and sentimental of me, that a magistrate cannot give a sentence longer than a year—or perhaps it is eighteen months. Lord knows, I did not find the Captain appetizing, but Mr. James is such a psychological cockroach that I doubt if I would have many qualms about stealing from him myself.

We were on our way out to go to a fitting at the tailor's when we met the detective this morning. Both my coat and Henry's suit are nearly finished, and I humbly eat my words *in re* Savile Row and the Acropolis. Henry and I together, in our new clothes, are going to present such a staggering aggregate of Quiet Worth as will have even the lions in Trafalgar Square twitching their tails and saying, "Whew!"

July 23rd

Henry—who, while he is in London, is doing a few errands and commissions for a publisher in New York—went off today to lunch with an editor in one of the big, pachydermic clubs near St. James's. I, in his absence, took the guide-book and went for an ambitious walk. (How I have *walked* since I have been in England! By the time I get home again, my feet are going to be of such a size that I will be able to have drawers put in them and use them for desks.) London surprises me by being so little like New York. Not that I expected skyscrapers, but I was unprepared to find the capital of the British Empire in effect a stepped-up Exeter. For all its roaring buses and tidal waves of traffic, London is only reluctantly and grudgingly modern. Backed into a corner and kicked in the stomach, it consents to put up a few electric signs around Piccadilly Circus, but its flair seems to be for piously conservative shops like Burberry's; for sedate, slow-breathing squares with an ampli-tude of park, generally private, in the middle; and for little streets as scowlingly attractive, though not so self-conscious, as etchings.

London's major aptitude, however, is for lav-ishly, easily, openhandedly interrupting all the most important places in town with public parks of arrogant extent and prodigal leafiness. A visitor so disposed could probably see most of central London by swinging from branch to branch. The moist climate (in a less charitable mood, I would have said soggy) accounts for the greenness and the air of full-fleshed abundance of these parks, but that they are so neat and un-littered must be due at least partly to the instinctive good manners and considerateness of the London population. Perhaps also the long love affair between Englishmen and the responsive English soil has something to do with it. Whatever it is, compared with the elderly-streetwalker aspect of New York parks, the parks of London look like prom dates.

July 24th

Henry came back in an exceedingly pleasant mood from his luncheon yesterday, having had good food and good wine and entertaining discourse. The man who sat next to him told him that England is a terrible country, but not nearly so bad as it is painted. I felt rather cast down at listening to Henry's report, for it made me realize how little point there is in a woman's keeping a diary in a country where the best food, the best clothes, the best clubs, the best conversation and practically all the liquor are for men.

Mr. James has taken to hanging around the hall again, and told us proudly that he was going to dismiss all the chambermaids, just in case they should have been in league with the Captain. Henry replied, in a voice that must have left a coating of icicles on his tonsils, that it seemed an extreme measure. As the chamber-maids are still here, I suppose the owner was merely making a desperate bid for attention.

The detective called on Henry this morning to ask if he would testify in court to having given Captain Featherstone rent money. I was not there, but Henry said that though he was extremely reluctant, he found himself exposed to such a barrage of tact and sympathy and courteous understanding that he had been out-maneuvered into saying yes before he had time to pull himself together.

"Why did they ask you?" I said. "Why didn't they get one of the other tenants?"

"Dunno," replied Henry lightly. "Maybe the others were all behind with their rent."

July 26th

We had a long conversation, in very friendly wise, with the detective this afternoon. He came to tell Henry what questions would be asked in court and what to say to them, and stayed to discuss the Lindbergh case (the conduct of which obviously shocked him deeply, though he was careful not to say so) and detective stories and English murder trials. Everything was going beautifully until I thoughtlessly asked him if he would take tea with us. In an instant all his poise and surety dropped away from him and he looked piteously upset. "Oh!" he exclaimed in a horrified voice, and added stammeringly that there was a chap waiting for him. Henry saved the situation by pretending to believe him implicitly, which somewhat restored the poor man to his professional calm. But the *esprit de corps* was shot to pieces and shortly afterwards Henry and I took our leave and went out.

"He *looks* good enough to eat with," I said defensively, as soon as we were out of the door.

"My dear," replied Henry in a reproachful voice, "here the English have gone to all this trouble to make the world unsafe for democracy, and you come along and try to spoil it. Didn't you notice," he added, "that he calls me 'sir'?"

July 27th

Henry lunched at another pachyderm today and I went shopping. London stores are not imposing. Most of their window displays look like jungles and even the pared-down ones lack intuition and rightness. And their idea of a well-turned-out woman is something resembling a Biblical character in a charade. But London salespeople are balm in Gilead. When I was little, I was afraid of the dark, but when I grew older, I learned to be afraid of salesgirls. They know by instinct, the unblessèd damozels, that I am no match for their contemptuous inflections. "Oh, boy!" they say, when they see me approaching, "here's where we unload that magenta was left over from 1926." In London, however, the salespeople take the merciful and soothing attitude that customers just drop in to say hello and any purchasing they may do on the side is merely a pleasant little irrelevancy. If this is Old World culture, I like it.

July 30th

Today was the day of Captain Featherstone's trial. Henry and I left for the court early in order to avoid being accompanied by Mr. James, who, though we treat him rather as if he were a culture of cholera germs, nevertheless shows a pronounced taste for our company. By the time the owner arrived, Henry and I were unassailably entrenched between a couple of policemen and he had to sit by himself. The courtroom was small and old, but extremely clean. The magistrate sat on a kind of small throne which was flanked with red velvet draperies, somewhat the worse for wear and inscribed in tarnished gilt with a royal insignia, I have forgotten exactly what. His Worship was a well-groomed and educated-looking man of about middle age, dishearteningly superior to the sort of people who usually occupy similar levels in American law. He looked kind in a seasoned way. I asked Henry what a man of such parts was doing in such a relatively humble legal position. "Probably *noblesse oblige*," he answered—which made the neighboring policeman glance at him uneasily.

There were a great many cases before the Captain's—old women haled in for drinking and fighting, boys charged with stealing fruit, fruit vendors charged with obstructing traffic with their barrows, women lodging complaints against their neighbors or against absent or alcoholic husbands, landlords bringing in tenants for non-payment of rent. The old woman drunk-and-disorderlies appeared to have the privileged standing of regular customers. The magistrate seemed especially well disposed toward them, and, indeed, the way in which those battered, toothless, caved-in old derelicts hoisted themselves into the dock and slewed around to face the judiciary was not only impenitent, it was downright impish.

The atmosphere of the court was definitely paternal, though there was a perceptible vein of no-nonsense underneath. A badly frightened young woman with a baby in her arms told a long and unintelligible story, the burden of which was that her husband was threatening to kill her. The magistrate said rather coldly that there was nothing he could do about it, but he told the constable who had escorted the woman in to have the husband brought round so that he could talk to him privately. Most of the cases were dismissed with a fine. The defendants, even the ones who had pleaded their causes with most urgency, accepted the fines philosophically. The rent cases took the longest, the magistrate investigating the means of the tenants with much care. In every case he gave them a long time in which to pay, and, judging from their resources, they must certainly have needed it.

Captain Featherstone's was the last case before lunch. The detective came over to us just before the prisoner was brought in and said that the ex-manager was going to plead guilty and no witnesses would be called. This was a relief to Henry, though it must have been a bitter pill for Mr. James. The poor Captain's affair was over in a few minutes. He was brought in, trying to hide as much of his meager little person as was possible in the shabby grey overcoat with which he was wrapped and looking so supremely wretched that it was indecent to watch him. I could not hear him when he said, "Guilty," his voice was so low. We learned, when the magistrate read aloud the notes on the case, that the Captain had not been a captain, but a lieutenant, in the army and that he had once before served six months for a similar offence. The magistrate had been dispassionate all along, but it seemed to me he was exceptionally impersonal about the Captain. He sentenced him to a year. The Captain sagged a little, so that he looked even smaller, and crept wordlessly out. The magistrate watched him carefully to the door, but it was impossible to tell from his face what he was thinking.

Everybody stood up, and Mr. James reached us in one bound. "You know," he said virtuously, cocking his eyebrows at the door through which the Captain had disappeared and speaking in a voice like canned sardines, "he drinks."

"So do I," said Henry sharply, and took advantage of the owner's instinctive recoil to let three or four substantial policemen get between him and us.

We took a hearty farewell of the detective, who seems to have forgiven me the tea incident and who left us his address in case he could ever do anything for us. We had planned to go to Simpson's and treat ourselves to a good lunch, as compensation for an especially semifluid dinner last night, but it was too much of a transition from the magistrate's court. We went to a Corner House instead, and postponed Simpson's until some day when our recollections of His Worship's clients should have gotten conveniently dimmed.

July 31st

Englishwomen's shoes look as if they had been made by someone who had often heard shoes described, but had never seen any, and the problem of buying shoes in London is almost insoluble—unless you pay a staggering tariff on American ones. What provokes this outburst is that I have just bought a pair of English bedroom slippers and I not only cannot tell the left foot from the right, but it is only after profound deliberation that I am able to distinguish between the front and the back.

August 2nd

Day after tomorrow we sail for Gothenburg, and meantime we are in Surrey, in the midst of a fragrantly leisurely English weekend. The following things are beautiful: the house, the countryside, the children, the dogs and the hostess. The host is not beautiful, but he is an amiable, uncomplicated and friendly gentleman who has lived and worked in almost every livable and workable corner of the world, an experience which has given him a gratifying pliancy of mind. The children are very little in evidence, but when they do appear, are so polite and courtly as to make me feel by contrast a veritable lumberjack. Better that, however, than the other way around. We all (except the children) go for walks, and when it begins to rain, come in and dawdle around a tall, white, Lady Clara Vere de Vere of a fireplace. Henry

No strain at all

and the others play games, during which I am generously allowed to read. I am no good at games, my mind—when it comes to playfulness and freedom of motion—being barely able to hold its own with a glacier.

I begin to understand, now, why English weekends are so long. They induce a definite state of mind and body which it is no more possible to put a stop to before it has run its course than it is suddenly and arbitrarily to wake one's self up out of a drugged sleep.

August 5th

Technically, we are en route to Gothenburg on the S.S. *Suecia*, but the statement is made only tentatively, as the *Suecia* seems to be doing its best to fling us off. The trouble is, of course, that the *Suecia* is one of your tall, thin, modern girls, with no hips to speak of, whereas the North Sea, at the moment, consists of nothing but hips.

"A pretty thought," says Henry. "At any other time. . . ."

Henry is keeping from being seasick by staying on deck and by sheer will power, both of which activities entail a severe strain. My system is to stay in bed with six detective stories and a quadruple order of brandy. It is no strain at all.

GOTHENBURG—I have been wandering around
the large, grey, immaculate corridors of the hotel trying to find the bathroom. ("Wandering"
is perhaps an understatement.) *Utgång* proved
to be the door to the fire escape. *Hiss* was the
elevator, though I tried it hopefully, thinking
perhaps they had onomatopoeia in Swedish. At
length a chambermaid, taking in the problem
at one glance, waved me upstairs, where I found
Damen and *Herren*.

After England, Gothenburg looks surprisingly
American. The automobiles are the same size as
ours, the houses are larger than English houses,
and the sun, instead of making one of its shy,
misty, English appearances, is shining boldly
and aggressively and as if no rain were contem-
plated for at least a week. Not, however, that
you would be likely to think yourself in an
American city. A good many of the streets and
squares are cobbled, there is a provocative and
all-pervasive smell of coffee, the railroad station
has rustic beams across the ceiling with potted
plants hanging from them, the pale-blue trolley
cars (with white canvas curtains at each end)
go about joined together, like copulating butter-
flies, and the streets and sidewalks are so clean
that you could throw a sofa cushion into the
gutter and settle down there without a qualm.

Spent most of the afternoon taking a walk. Remembering English shops, I thought the Gothenburg stores bright-eyed and unapologetic. We had dinner in a terraced and balconied restaurant standing in the middle of a park. The park is more than presentable, but its flowers look pale and stringy compared with the flowers in English parks. The waiter at the restaurant spoke only Swedish, and the "Meals" section of the phrase book was evidently compiled by a pregnant woman with a larger than usual assortment of whims. But by ordering on a blind chance, we got an exquisite if anonymous mixture, apparently composed of chicken and fish and cheese, and a piece of iced canteloupe for which a well-advised Greek god would have traded in a week's allowance of ambrosia.

I am going to like this country.

August 7th

We are on a boat which goes all the way across Sweden from Gothenburg to Stockholm by a series of rivers and lakes and canals, taking three days for the trip. It is a fat little boat—so distended, in fact, that it can barely pull itself around into a point at the prow. The dining room is minute; the passengers go into the cabins like buttons into buttonholes; and walking along the corridors is somewhat akin to being digested. But everything which is not fresh white paint is polished plate glass, and it is comfortable, even though you do sometimes feel like a fraction which is being reduced to its lowest terms.

The passengers are a mixture of nationalities. At our table in the dining room is a Frenchman traveling with his two daughters. The Frenchman's face scampers when he talks. One of the daughters is vividly beautiful, with curly auburn hair and heroic teeth. She is satiny and fluid enough to ripple, if you threw a stone at her, and when she comes into the dining salon, every man in the room sits bolt upright and begins to run the tip of his tongue over his lips. Daughter is not by any means unaware of this reaction, but Papa first glares at her and then baptizes all the surrounding males with a glance of electric dislike. Daughter drops sullenly into her seat; all the men pick up menus and say hastily to their wives, "What will you have, dear?"; Papa with a happy smile begins to order; and the dining room subsides into monogamy again.

In addition to the French family there is also a family of Danes, a regiment of them, all blond, all smiling, and all stamped with an unmistakable family resemblance. The table next to us in the dining room accommodates a very elderly Norwegian. He has his meat cut up for him by his wife, and his thin legs are bowed outward under the weight of his pear-shaped, dropsical torso like struggling industries trying to carry watered stock. His wife, a German, scrapes her iron-grey hair into a large bun at the back, and with "Let us have peace" carved across her diaphragm, she would make a very passable understudy for Grant's Tomb. When we sit down, she exchanges a few cast-iron amenities with Henry, who speaks German, and tonight she even went so far as to compliment him, grudgingly, on his accent. She does not speak to anyone else, and her husband, so far, has not spoken at all.

Among the Anglo-Saxon contingent is a pathetic English couple from Bournemouth—a tired little man sagging under his burden of vigorous tweeds and a woman who wears girlish pink or blue gingham dresses and ties pink or blue ribbons around her hair, but obviously from weariness and force of habit rather than any hope of convincing people. We talk to them a good deal, partly because there are so few English-speaking people on the boat and partly because they are so small and helpless and unprotected. Also on board is a young man from Princeton, traveling with twenty-two suitcases and a four-inch coating of aristocratic indifference. He was clearly designed by nature to be pushed overboard, and I feel slightly blasphemous every time I go past without even jostling him.

August 8th

I have spent most of the day sitting on a pile of freight in the prow baking in the sunlight. After two months in England, good strong sunlight that begins in the morning and continues without interruption until evening seems like a work of art. But the recollection of English countryside makes the big, green, unpopulated Swedish landscape—which is almost all woods and which keeps reminding me of America— look unwrought-upon and rather monotonously virginal. Occasionally we come to stretches of gently-rolling farming country where the farm buildings are square and ungraceful and generally painted red and the farms have an air of restrained prosperity. There are locks almost hourly. If the locks happen to be near a farm, little girls in Swedish costume come down to watch the boat, and the passengers rush to the rail to photograph them. The little girls submit to the photography with the exaggerated calm of an adult getting ready to tell an excited adolescent that this is just a stage he is going through.

Later

Late this afternoon, in the middle of a vast stretch of forest, the boat stopped at a landing

—*designed by Nature to be pushed overboard*

stage about the size of a conductor's podium and by some freakish chance which no one could explain, thirteen middle-aged women from California got on. They were good-natured as they streaked around, dividing up cabins and finding lost gloves and borrowing aspirin, but their voices were like trolley wheels going around a curve. The poor little couple from Bournemouth cowered in a corner. The young Princetonian detached himself from the railing —where he had been standing in a graceful attitude most of the day, inviting his manifest destiny—and said, "Well, really. . . ." Giving the unconscious ladies a glance which was the social equivalent of the winter at Valley Forge, he went forward and began ostentatiously digging the twenty-two suitcases out from under the tarpaulin which had been respectfully draped over them.

Unfortunately for the Princetonian, however, the California ladies eventually did settle down quietly on the afterdeck with their knitting and a generous cud of obstetrical folklore. But by that time the young man had already informed the Captain and a few favored friends that he was getting off at eleven o'clock at Lynköping (pronounced, happily, Lynchirping) and going on to Stockholm by train. We are now getting close to Lynköping and our collegian looks tired —the unexpected quiescence of the Californians saddled him with the difficult problem of looking aloof for four or five hours when there was nothing to look aloof from. But I daresay it was good practice for him and will come in handy some day.

LYNKÖPING—We got off at Lynköping last night too, as it turned out that two of the California ladies had reserved our cabin, which we had not. We are taking the train to Stockholm this afternoon. Lynköping is a clean, cobbled town, filled with big and somewhat bald-looking houses. As a matter of fact, there is something in the handsome inexpressiveness of Swedish architecture and Swedish towns which suggests a very good-looking face without any eyebrows.

Later

An excellent lunch, mostly from a smörgåsbord table which was a sort of culinary Venusberg. Swedish coffee, incidentally, is better than American and infinitely better than English. The English do themselves proud with tea, and their tea makes ours seem like a distillation of red blotting paper. But English coffee tastes the way a long-standing family joke sounds, when you try to explain it to outsiders, and they serve it with boiled milk instead of cream. The skin is always conscientiously left in the boiled milk, so that when you stir the completed fluid, bits of white membrane swirl filmily around the spoon.

Later

STOCKHOLM—We arrived here around four o'clock this afternoon and are staying at a hotel which occupies two floors in what was formerly a mansion and is now a business building. Our room looks like something out of a Graustark romance. Five tall French windows open on a balcony; the big white double doors, with their movie-of-love-and-intrigue handles, go all the way up to the ceiling; and in one corner a white porcelain stove also reaches to the ceiling, though the stove is apparently vestigial, as there are radiators. The beds are as large as picnic grounds, and whenever I catch sight of the chandelier, which is of gold and crystal, I pat myself nervously to make sure I do not have the plans of West Point down the front of my dress.

The manager of the hotel, however, is anything but Graustarkian, being a short, solid, grey little man whose face is so absolutely blank and impassive that all it needs is a letterhead. He speaks English extremely well, almost without an accent, but he did not answer our polite sallies except when it was unavoidable. Nevertheless, after we had unpacked, he offered to take us to a park called Skansen, where there is an outdoor museum of old Swedish houses. And on the trolley going out to Skansen, he unbent sufficiently to tell us that his name is Pedersen, after which he dwelt—with a heavy infatuation which resisted all our efforts to switch to a livelier topic—on the routes and schedules of the various Stockholm trolley lines.

The houses of the outdoor museum are small, and the dark interiors, livened up with carved wood and bright stitching and vivid-colored paint, seem snug and peasant-like. They do, at least, to one whose knowledge of peasants derives largely from department store advertising. But after we had seen half a dozen houses, and had watched, from the outside of a thick ring of people, a few flashes of tossing skirts and embroideries where folk dancing was going on, I began to get tired. We had had a long walk over the cobblestones of Lynköping in the morning. I suggested to Mr. Pedersen that I had had enough, but his only reply was slowly to turn his face on me and slowly to turn it away again (it was like a barn door moving in the wind). Then he led the way to another house.

Henry habitually walks as if he were tired, so I did not realize that he was folding up too until he made a face at Mr. Pedersen, stalking ahead of us, and said, "Boots, boots, marching up and down again," in an only half-joking voice. At that I plucked up my courage and told the manager point-blank that I was too tired to go any further. I thought he had not heard me, and was just about to say it again, when he announced with sepulchral calm, "We will finish." I was afraid to rebel. It seemed to me quite within the realm of possibility that Mr. Pedersen would merely take me by the hair and carefully and methodically drag me through the rest of the exhibits. We went on. When the manager was not looking, Henry and I sat down surreptitiously in ingle nooks and closet beds and ovens, and when he stopped to point out, in his deep, judicial voice, something of especial interest, we stood on one foot and waggled the other, blissfully savoring the release from pressure.

Eventually, it did end, though not before the manager had thrown in, for good measure, a herd of dusty reindeer and an encampment of Lapps. Mr. Pedersen turned to us with a tiny smile and said that we had seen everything. I joggled Henry and he woke up and said, "Thank you." The manager tipped his hat and walked away, and Henry and I virtually fell into a big, wide-windowed restaurant which stood on a slope nearby.

"I suppose," I said guiltily, as we finished the hors d'œuvres, "we should have asked Mr. Pedersen to have dinner with us."

"No," replied Henry unperturbed, "he'd

have made us eat the olive pits and the tails of
the sardines."

August 10th

I had heard Stockholm called the Venice of
the North, but I did not realize that it would
have so much water in it, or that it would be
completely ringed in with forests. Both Lake
Mälaren and Saltsjön, an arm of the Baltic, go
through violent contortions in order to get at as
much of the city as possible, and you can hardly
walk two blocks without seeing hundreds of
boats—from the *Gripsholm*, anchored off Skansen
when we were there yesterday, to the skiffs
under the Opera House and the King's palace,
where men bring up crayfish in huge, circular
nets. When it comes to civic self-respect, Stockholm makes New York seem like an Iroquois
village. It does not, as we saw when we took a
trolley car which goes all the way around its
circumference, trail wretchedly off into shanties
and little houses of heartbreaking ugliness. It
just stops, and the woods begin. Sometimes it
stops with a final flourish of cooperative apartment houses for workmen—neat, new-looking
buildings ranged along the tops of cliffs with the
omnipresent Swedish forests at their back doors.

One reads that there are no slums in Stockholm, and certainly there are no slums that can
be discovered in a single day of looking for them.

This afternoon we took a ferry to Södermalm, which the guidebook says is the working- and middle-class quarter. Södermalm, too, is on top of a cliff, and what we saw of it was extremely clean. In some places, the buildings are long in the tooth and rather sad-looking, but nothing we came across could even remotely be called a slum. The feel of Stockholm is humorless, and you get the impression, in those parts of the city lying somewhat away from the center of town, that there is a stiff-necked, potted-plant-and-clean-apron element of formidable dimensions. But the odor of sanctity is mitigated by the bright, sharp smell of coffee, and riding and walking and taking ferries around Stockholm, you grow more and more convinced that *this* is what is meant by civilization.

Later

One of the first things that struck me when I went to England was how many more War memorials there are than at home. In Sweden, the entire absence of monuments with 1917 or 1914–1918 on them makes you feel light and unclouded and almost irresponsible.

August 11th

We have breakfast in our Graustark room in the mornings, with all five windows standing open to the vigorous Swedish sunlight. A big,

Wagnerian maid brings a big, Wagnerian pot of coffee, and there is heavy cream and sweet butter and a basket full of hot rolls. After breakfast Mr. Pedersen comes in with hypnotic suggestions about what we ought to do during the day. If Mr. Pedersen knows that he is living in a country at which wistful liberals of other nations goggle with envy, he gives absolutely no sign of it. The only facial expression he permits himself is a glow of discontent when Henry or I say anything in praise of Sweden or Swedish life. In telling us about things that are worth seeing or doing in Stockholm, his manner is that of a conscientious doctor prescribing for a routine and uninteresting illness.

This afternoon, at Mr. Pedersen's suggestion, we took a motorboat excursion around the city. The other passengers were all Americans, most of them sober-seeming people, some with copies of *Sweden, The Middle Way* under their arms. But the two women who sat in front of Henry and me would, considered as compatriots, have brought a blush of shame to the cheek of the Great Stone Face. They did not know each other, but quickly introduced themselves ("I'm from Cleveland," one of them kept saying fretfully) and began to talk about Europe as if it were one long series of bargains in scarfs.

The boat started, and a tall, blond young man—they grow on trees in this country—with a mellow, intelligent voice, took his place in the front and began pointing out the places we were passing. The sun shone on the varnish of the boat; the passengers held their hats in the breeze; on either hand the buildings of Stockholm engaged in their unequal struggle with cliffs and trees and water; and the Sober Element eyed the young guide attentively.

After a while somebody timidly asked a question about the cooperative apartments, then more questions were asked, and soon the young man was being pelted with requests for figures and percentages and statistics.

Into this discussion the lady from Cleveland came like a hand grenade.

"Cooperatives . . .," she said to her seatmate, in the purposely loud voice of one who has been introduced to a tame centipede and asked to pet it.

The Sober Element jumped, and everybody craned to look at the speaker. A wizened little man with a beautiful head of silver hair said quite audibly to his wife, "If she doesn't like it here, why doesn't she go back where she came from?"

A little, breathy sound of laughter ran over the boat. The lady from Cleveland sat up straighter and took a fresh grip on her pocketbook.

"You think you're funny, don't you?" she said.

The young guide quickly made his face enigmatic and began to speak again. The little silver-haired man had not even turned around.

The guide's lecture flowed evenly on. People looked at the buildings he pointed out and sometimes wrote things down on bits of paper, but no more questions were asked. Suddenly, however, there was another interruption. The guide had just made a polite but rather vague reference to President Roosevelt.

"Only the niggers like *him*," said the lady from Cleveland, in a tone so loaded with hatred that another sentence would have sunk the boat.

The guide looked perplexed, and in the silence the rapid thudding of the boat's motor sounded very loud. The trip began all at once to seem oppressively long-drawn-out.

A second time the young man took up his lecture. After a long while, and by degrees, the Sober Element forgot about the lady from Cleveland and began to ask questions again. It was nearly the end of the trip when the lecturer got around to speaking of prisons, and told us that capital punishment had been abolished in Sweden.

The lady who was not from Cleveland was better-natured than her seatmate.

"In our country," she announced cheerfully,

"we think we don't have enough capital punishment."

The Sober Element sat perfectly still, but the
atmosphere of the boat could have been negoti-
ated with a Flexible Flyer. The lady from Cleveland noticed it immediately, and folded in her
lips as if someone had suggested taking them
away from her. The lady who was not from
Cleveland only smiled modestly to herself.

The boat lolloped gently up to the dock.

The Sober Element continued to sit still
while the lady from Cleveland, followed by her
still smiling companion, ascended with unneces-
sary firmness the steps of the pier. As the two
women walked away, the little silver-haired
man looked musingly after them, gave himself
a sort of shake, and said, "Harpies!"

We all smiled uncertainly at each other and
began to scramble out of the boat.

August 12th

The famous Town Hall of Stockholm is a
curious, unforgettable combination of romance
—not lyricism, but romance—with discipline.
The building stands on the tip of an island,
with water on two sides. Constructed of specially
made brick, it is a deep red in color, a soft but
powerful shade, with more blue in it than the
old Tudor bricks of English walls and houses.
The building surrounds a big open courtyard,

117

and one corner of the structure goes up, unsurprisingly, into a tall, slightly tapering, faintly Dutch-looking tower. The courtyard is uneven and slopes irregularly down to one side, where, through a grey loggia, you look out over a grass terrace to Lake Mälaren. Not twelve feet from the edge of the terrace, little white boats cut through the water like small boys on absorbing errands. They seem so close that it would be only mildly startling if one of them wheeled quickly and came up into the courtyard.

The Town Hall, though there is no large recognition when you first look at it, is full of smaller recognitions. Every device from Flemish carvings to Moorish arches has been used in the ornamentation, but used so sparingly that they are all caught up and held in suspension, as it were, in the calm, plain vastness of the red brick. The guiding principle of modern Swedish design seems to be an initial plainness which, on second glance, is full of small, nourishing irregularities. We noticed the same thing yesterday at an exhibition of ceramics.

The ceramics exhibition was at one of the big department stores, and when we were there, an American woman—so old and so patrician that she ought to have been specially lighted and kept under glass—was buying the vase which I thought the most beautiful one on view. She paid for her purchase and gave her name and allowed her eyeglasses to skip back to their little gold button on her shoulder.

"And now," she said to the salesgirl, with the fanatic sparkle of a person who has finished the cake and is ready for the icing, "show me the counter where Garbo worked."

August 13th

We take the night train to Oslo tomorrow, and it will be a wrench to leave. I go about Stockholm with the veins standing out on my forehead in the effort not to be foolishly enthusiastic and to remember that there must be a catch in it somewhere. But the city has the overwhelming beauty of common sense—it is the kind of city you would have for yourself, if you knew a little dressmaker who could run you up one. In the time we have been here, we have not seen a single one of the suffocatingly pitiful human wrecks who crawl along the streets of London and New York. Stockholm has its dull, bleak spots, of course, though not many of them. But they are not festering with poverty, and the traveler can go in and out of and around the city without seeing houses or people that make him curl up at the edges. Definitely, it takes a longer stay than ours to be disillusioned about this town, even with the best will in the world.

The restaurants—with, possibly, the Town

Hall thrown in on the side—constitute an entirely adequate reason for coming three thousand miles, even if one should see nothing at all of the rest of Europe. Almost always big, they are sunlit in the daytime and well lighted at night, and the patrons, of both sexes, show a gratifying disposition to be beautiful and blond. The best meal in town costs a dollar and a half, and by omitting the flossier courses, it is to be had for seventy-five cents. There is no smörgåsbord—that admirable custom is going out in the cities, Mr. Pedersen says, and survives only in rural districts—but the cuisine is a thing which cannot be described without descending to the phraseology of amateur sonnets and travel booklets.

The way in which I respond like a plucked lyre to Swedish food and comfort and cleanliness and general soundness makes me realize how desperately unadventurous and middle class I am. I suppose I ought to be used by this time to being myself, but sometimes it comes as rather a shock.

Later

Hearing music again, after not having heard any for a long time, you feel as if you had two pairs of ears. We have just come back from *Carmen*. The orchestra handled the Spanish music punctiliously, but a little reproachfully. The staging was done as a series of tableaux, extremely effective at first, but acquiring a wearisome, watch-the-birdie quality during the progress of the scenes. However, the Carmen and the Escamillo reached down and yanked the performance up to the proper temperamental level. They both sang extraordinarily well, and the Carmen, in particular, had a voice like dark Irish honey—though it was not nearly large enough to have filled the Metropolitan. She was, in addition, beautiful, and her smile was something to find your way with in the dark: but she had one serious fault. Though not a particularly large woman, she was extremely ungraceful and trundled around like an excavating machine.

August 14th

We have just had dinner with the young guide who was on the motorboat excursion the other day, Henry having concluded that it would be a shame to let an English-speaking and obviously intelligent Swede slip through our fingers. Mr. Brandt is a nineteen-year-old college student who seems much older than that. He has impeccable manners, and his vagrant, trans-European childhood as the son of a newspaper correspondent has given him a poise which is equal to anything short of actual nitroglycerin. He and Henry, in fact, sat at the table being calm at each other until the evening felt like a lagoon.

Young Mr. Brandt has exactly Mr. Pedersen's you-don't-know-the-half-of-it attitude about Sweden, except that he is laughingly rueful where Mr. Pedersen is merely sour. *Sweden, The Middle Way*, Mr. Brandt believes, paints too favorable a picture. Perhaps it does, though certainly one would not be inclined to think so from a week's visit. But Mr. Brandt's arguments against the book are vague and general and not very well implemented, and I suspect he is, to some extent anyway, only suffering a natural reaction from meeting three boatloads a day of Mr. Childs' readers.

There is a small group of Swedish Nazis, according to Mr. Brandt—including some at the University of Uppsala, where he is a student— but he says they are not growing in number. Nevertheless, he claims that most Swedes know that Sweden will be in the next war, on Germany's side. Swedes, says Mr. Brandt good-humoredly, are dull company. Mebbe so. It would not surprise me. But they have an instinct for human dignity which makes their country exhilarating.

We leave Sweden without having had nearly enough of it, and with a large burden of unsatisfied curiosity, only an equally urgent curiosity about the Norwegian fjords prodding us on. Not knowing the Swedish language is a handicap, but not knowing the literature is a severer one. Messrs. Brandt and Pedersen emerge from nothingness and we have no pattern, however tentative, into which to fit them. When you go to England, on the other hand, all the stock characters you have been reading about all your life—from Her Grace, the Dowager Duchess, down to Honest Jack, the British Workman—are lined up on the dock to meet you.

August 15th

OSLO—We should have come here first, and then gone to Stockholm, because after Stockholm, Oslo seems anticlimactic. It is beautiful enough, with a fjord to its credit and hills, bearded like infidels, sloping steeply down to the water. And there are almost as many small white boats as there are in Stockholm, though they are in the harbor in front of the town, and not inextricably mixed up with the main parts of the city, like the Stockholm boats. But either the coffee is bad, and the food tastes of sour milk, and the streets look sloppy and careless in comparison with Swedish streets, and the town smells of cold grease, or else I—disgruntled, and homesick for Stockholm—am imagining all these shortcomings.

In three days we start on a trip through the

mountains and fjords to the northwest, ending up at Bergen, from which we sail for England. A travel agency called Bennett's, which specializes in Norway and seems to know the country pine needle by pine needle, has planned the trip and made all the arrangements. People who always manage to see the real France and the real Italy and the real 181st Street and Amsterdam Avenue look down on planned itineraries; but a competent-sounding book called *Norway On Ten Pounds* points out that this country is peculiarly difficult to travel through singlehanded, on account of the steepness of the mountains. It recommends Bennett's for soft-boned and slack-fibered travelers, which is an almost photographic description of Henry and me. Particularly me.

August 16th

I was walking through the hotel corridor this afternoon, on my way to the elevator, when somebody in the ladies' toilet shot the bolt with a noise like a gun going off, clawed open the door, and hurled herself into my path with so much force as to knock me up against the wall.

"Do you speak English?" she demanded. She was a fat, pursy little woman. Her accent was English and her tone was that of an exasperated Grand Duchess addressing a journeyman exterminator.

"A little," I replied.

"It flooded," she said furiously. "I mean, it actually flooded! I was just standing there, and when I . . ."—she gulped and glared at me—"when I pulled the chain . . ."—her voice rose to a thin howl—"it went all over!"

I suddenly realized that from the half-open door of the toilet there issued the sound as of a giant gargling.

"Tell the management," I suggested sympathetically.

"Tell the management!" She tore the words away from me. "I certainly *will* tell the management! But what good will *that* do?"

She paused and rummaged in the slimy depths of her vocabulary.

"Foreigners!" she said.

"No doubt," I answered, not knowing what else to say.

She looked at me with a little start.

"Of course, it was all right," she said hastily, in a calmer tone. "Of course, it was all right. But suppose one had been, uh . . . suppose one had been, uh . . . suppose-one-had-been-BUSY!"

August 17th

We are too late and too far south for the midnight sun, but it would have been the midnight rain anyway, yesterday and today. Fortunately, the two things I like most about Oslo are indoors—the Grand Hotel café and the haunting, incredible Viking ships. The sandwiches at the Grand Hotel café have bottoms but no tops, and in my Index of Lucullan Pleasures, they have shouldered their way right up to the level of Stockholm food. The Viking ships, like the sandwiches, also have bottoms but no tops. Dug up in various places around the Oslofjord, they are housed in a building specially put up for them on a peninsula across the harbor from the town. There are three of them, and they are painted black. One is a ruin, one is only half ruined, and one is complete. About seventy feet long and with places for sixteen pairs of oars, they are slightly too large and unwieldy for a Water Carnival at a girls' camp; but the imagination, called on to picture them in the North Atlantic, simply puts a "Closed For Alterations" sign on the door and goes home for the day.

August 18th

ULVIK—I feel as if I had done more traveling today than in all the rest of the summer put together, and we have looked at enough scenery to carry us through, even if we should have to spend the rest of our lives viewing barbed wire and flights of subway stairs.

We left Oslo by train at ten o'clock and got off at a place called Haugastöl at four. The Oslo-Bergen railway goes northwest over the mountain tops. Once in a while we saw fierce little valleys scuttling furtively around the corner, but valleys do not seem to be much thought of in these parts of Norway. It rained during the whole trip. There was no mist, though, and we could see clearly. Outside of Oslo the mountains are steep and covered to the top with such a heavy growth of timber that it looks from the train window as if you could barely get your clenched fist in between the trees. By lunch time, the mountains had begun to have outrageous crags on the top, and far below we occasionally saw a narrow streak of water. In another hour, we were above the timber line and moving across brown, scarred land, strewn with boulders and bleak as the end of a love affair. In the middle distance, brown mountains were heaped around like portions of cold pudding, and we heard the other people in the car—they were all Americans or English—say that the white streaks on the mountains were glaciers.

The car, instead of having compartments, was arranged like an American Pullman. Across the aisle from us were two young American Jews, expensively dressed and accompanied by expensive luggage. One of them was pudgy and talkative—the sort of man who, as a baby, was called a fat rascal and who has not changed materially in growing up. The other, who was silent and seemed the older of the two, had a delicate, antique face drawn like a thin, dark veil across his mind.

When they got on at Oslo, the older young man was in the process of discovering that the porter did not understand German. Pudgy addressed his companion crisply, but not unkindly.

"Save time you just sit still and let him read your mind," he said.

When we came back from lunch, Pudgy was remarking whimsically, "Landscape is cows, but scenery is when it looks like it was going to fall down on you."

The young men did not seem anxious to talk, and it was not until half an hour before we got off that we had any conversation with them. When the train pulled into Haugastöl, Pudgy shook hands with us both.

"We would of spoke to you sooner," he said, "but"—his voice made the apology for him— "we thought you was English."

An old Studebaker touring car met us at Haugastöl and we drove for two hours across a grey-green plateau called the Hardangervidda. At length we stopped and the driver waved to us to get out. Right in front of the car was a gorge whose size and black rocks and general bearing contained the raw material of two or three dozen blue-ribbon nightmares. It had stopped raining, and the driver rolled up the curtains of the car. We got in again and began to go down into the gorge. The road went through tunnels and around hairpin turns, but mostly it ran along little ledges with wholesale lots of nothingness underneath. We arrived at the bottom and found a fjord which made the one at Oslo look wide and tame and squatty; a boat which ran with a small whimpering noise; and half a skyful of sunset. By this time it was about half-past seven. As we started down the fjord, I looked at the dark green water and the black mountains thundering straight down into it and the sky pink with sunset overhead. Henry looked at it too.

"It's so simple and so violent," he said. "I feel as if I'd gotten into a child's drawing."

At ten o'clock, in a grey dusk, we arrived at Ulvik.

August 19th

Ulvik is a good deal like Eidfjord, where we took the boat last night. The village stands at the edge of the fjord, on a green and amiable slope, with mountains leaning over its shoulder and breathing down its neck. This morning being beautiful and sunny, Henry and I climbed a little way up the mountain in back of the hotel. At the last house in the village we came to a silky white goat who ate grass from my hand with a mildly patronizing air. This mountain is some-

what gentler than its neighbors, but above the
village, the path began clambering across semi-
vertical meadows and through plunging woods.
When we sat down to rest, in a field full of blue-
bells, we slid downward a few inches every time
we moved. The view across the sliver of fjord
to the crowding mountains was magnificent,
and we stayed and looked at it for so long that
if views wore away in the using, there would be
only about half of it left.

I shall always associate Ulvik with the sen-
sation of going downhill, my feet jammed up
into the toes of my shoes.

It began to rain again after lunch, but this is
a good hotel for a rainy day, having a sort of
rustic-modern interior, with titanic fires in the
fireplaces and the best smörgåsbord table so far,
not even excepting the Swedish ones.

August 20th

FLAAM—We went by auto this morning—another ancient American touring car—from Ulvik to Voss. It was a cold drive, and the more
I shrank into my clothes, the looser and further
off they seemed, but the road went through
pines and past lakes and waterfalls and down
ravines and under snarling peaks. Voss is a disconsolate, grey-brown little town, ringed in, at
some distance, by brown mountains. Standing
on the station platform, we suddenly heard

130

Henry's name being shrieked, and turning around, discovered the Father Abraham of all the touring cars, filled with fifteen-year-old girls from a school in which Henry used to teach. There is something in my contention that Henry is getting sufficiently round-shouldered to be recognized at five hundred yards purely through his leapfrog stance.

We took the train from Voss to a station called Myrdal. The line climbs all the way and goes above the timber line again, but there are so many tunnels and snowsheds that looking out of the window gets tedious. The passengers were nearly all English or American—in fact, we have heard English almost uninterruptedly ever since we left Oslo. It is, of course, a most "unreal" Norway that we are seeing, but in his fjord country there does not seem to be much "real" Norway to see. Here and there, in the infrequent valley bottoms, are shabby, untidy little farms where old women and children pile up the newly mown hay on vertical racks, and high up on the shoulders of the mountains you occasionally see a square of green, with a fleck of a house on it, where the farmers' wives are pasturing the cattle for the summer. But the country obviously cannot support more than the merest garnish of population.

It was cloudy but not raining when we got off at Myrdal, which was fortunate, as we were met by an open carriage. Two ponies drew the carriage. They were a dark cream color, with short, stiff manes, beautiful flowing tails, and brown eyes limpid and pleading enough to draw spurts of baby-talk from a public executioner. After a short drive, we stopped for lunch at a big hotel set in the midst of some lavish desolation and having an all-white dining room which looked like a clinic. Lunch over, we got into the carriage again and began to descend the Flaam Valley. The descent took most of the afternoon. I had thought the trip from the Hardangervidda down to Eidfjord was frightening, but that was a mere preliminary flourish, an inconsequential prelude, to the twenty-thousand-volt apprehension I felt in parts of the Flaam Valley.

The road was about four feet wide on the straightaway (if that is not too strong a word) and six feet wide on the turns. The driver put iron locks on the wheels, and sometimes he got out and walked, and sometimes Henry and I got out and walked too. I leapt out at every opportunity and was reluctant to get back in. But the driver, when I signalled that I wanted to keep on walking, said, "Ugh!" in the tone of one who is confronted with a veritable abyss of moral degeneracy. I had an abyss or two of my own to think about, but I got back in again. Henry pointed out that it must be entirely safe, as babes unborn and delicate old ladies are driven down the Flaam Valley every day all summer long. However, my talents do not seem to lie in the direction of jogging placidly along with God-knows-how-many thousand feet of sheer rock above and an equal quantity, unfenced, below. When a stone came rattling down from the cliff overhead and one of the ponies shied, a chill took hold of my spine like a lion getting in the groundwork on an early Christian martyr.

Later

The hotel at Flaam is damp and smells strongly of horses, but this end of the valley is a bright green and reassuring place, though the walls of rock on either side take your breath away and threaten never to bring it back again. The grass in these Norwegian valleys is even greener than English grass. Nature, in these parts, does nothing by halves.

Later

It is nine o'clock and grown dark and we have just finished supper. Norwegian food is, I think, noticeably inferior to Swedish, though after we left Oslo it stopped tasting as if it had been made with the milk from porcupines. Breakfast has a smörgåsbord table, and in addition the waitresses bring around coffee and boiled eggs. The midday meal is at two o'clock. It consists of soup; boiled potatoes and fish; boiled potatoes and meat; dessert and coffee—no smörgåsbord and, instead of bread and butter, thin crackers of rye flour. The evening meal is at eight o'clock. Boiled potatoes and meat, and then you go to the smörgåsbord table for anything else you want, including dessert. My premonition in Oslo about Norwegian coffee turns out to be right. It is bad.

Later

A restless evening. Henry is reading, but I have finished the only book I have with me and am not sleepy enough to go to bed. A boatload of tourists arrived a few minutes ago—Flaam is on a fjord. Everything in Norway is on a fjord. I went out and took a turn in the hotel's tiny garden, but the rampart of mountain looming up over it, darker than the darkness, made me feel about four inches high. And every time I looked at it, it seemed to me that it had moved a little nearer.

August 21st

BALESTRAND—We reached here by what, on a sunny day and in a less crowded boat, would have been a magnificent trip. But it rained all the way, and the hapless passengers had to choose between being squashed and asphyxiated in the cabin or squashed and dripped upon on the deck. We all, however, behaved exemplarily, and passed around chocolate and shared the edges of seats and apologized for treading on toes. Mother was *proud* of her little ladies and gentlemen.

We changed boats in the middle of the fjord. Two other boats suddenly appeared from around corners which no one had suspected were there and floated up to ours. One was lashed to each side of ours, and there followed a sort of pirate scene, as everybody swarmed over the railings. Everything had settled down, and the deck hands on our new boat were beginning to cast off, when a little woman who had been nosing like an excited puppy around the skyscraper of luggage on the forward deck, started to scream shrilly that her suitcase was not there. Stony-faced, the deck hands dismembered the whole pile of baggage, while everyone on all three boats watched. The missing piece was found at the very bottom. Everybody—except the deck hands—smiled, a few people laughed, and the plaintiff disappeared into the cabin, her face looking as if it had just been handed to her and she did not know how it was supposed to work.

Later

There is an American family at this hotel who were at the hotel in Ulvik. They say they have been told that the Norwegian summer really

ends August 15th and that we should have come
earlier. We keep running into people we have
encountered before on this Norwegian trip, and
as a matter of fact, the tourists seem to constitute
a closed corporation which has temporarily
taken over the whole fjord district. The few Nor-
wegians we see appear to regard us all as an act
of God, a housebroken avalanche which has
been trained to wire ahead when it is coming.
Incidentally, the impassivity of these Norwegian
drivers and porters and hotel clerks makes the
dead-panning of a well-trained English do-
mestic look like tinsel attitudinizing.

August 22nd

The fjord is wide at Balestrand, and the
mountains on the other side, being further
away, seem less overwhelming. But it has rained
all day and we have been hotel-bound. It is a
large hotel, furnished in a style which combines
Norwegian with Cigar Band. The gigantic desk
clerk wears a blue coachman's coat, and the
waitresses are dressed in the national costume.
In the lobby, tall showcases display Viking ship
ash trays and dusty jars of Elizabeth Arden
Muscle Cream. I suspect the management of
having ordered the Muscle Cream under the
impression that it was meant for bruised moun-
tain-climbers.

The big salons are filled with slippery brown

136

leather chairs, and on a table which looks as if Pithecanthropus Erectus might come crawling out from under it at any moment, the hotel library is neatly laid out. The library consists of the complete works of Henrik Ibsen (in Norwegian), several copies of a newspaper called the *Stavanger Aftenblad*, and a battered volume entitled *A Fjord Romance*. *A Fjord Romance* has a colored frontispiece of two lovers, dressed in the fashions of the early 1900's, exchanging liquid glances and failing to note that a large avalanche has reached a point six feet behind them. The walls of the salons are blanketed with amateur oil paintings. All but a handful of them portray the midnight sun, and some of the artists have been so carried away by their subject that the results look like colored diagrams of tonsillectomies.

Here and there people are playing card games, and enough knitting is going on to staff three or four guillotines working at capacity, but the tourists are not happy. The fjord side of the hotel is almost solid plate glass, and with the rain streaming down upon it, the rooms look cold and unprotected. In the corners, shifting from one foot to the other and smelling of wet wool, stand Les Miserables who have been out for a walk in spite of the rain and have returned to find the single fireplace monopolized by

137

heat-flushed old ladies whose friends save their places for them when they go into the dining room to eat.

Periodically, there is a mass movement towards the bar, but it is soon dissipated. The sale of hard liquor is illegal in Norway, and the glasses of sherry served by the hotel, though they are twice as large as ordinary portions, have no effect on the human frame at all, except to pucker the mouth until it feels as crowded as a lady's workbag. Dinner comes in the middle of the day, but the English tourists dress for supper. The dinner-jacketed Englishmen are regarded with wistful attentiveness by the American women, but the American men look at them with a glance which is not very far removed from "Yah! Momma's boy!"

The long day, wriggling imperceptibly forward through the rain, has gotten on everybody's nerves, and we will all be glad to move on tomorrow.

August 23rd

STALHEIM—This day by boat and touring car to Stalheim. In the rain. From here we go to Bergen. I was afraid, before we started out, that we had not allowed time enough for the fjord country. But even with good weather, a week would be enough. One fjord is much like another, and there is a limit to how long I, at least, can go on enjoying the feeling that a mile above my head ten thousand tons of rock are quivering gently in anticipation and murmuring to each other, "Hot dog, folks! Here comes Peg Halsey, after all these years."

August 24th

Stalheim is the wildest and craggiest of all. The hotel is like the one at Ulvik, and has everything a traveler could ask for in the way of open fires and smörgåsbord, but instead of being on a fjord, it is on top of a jagged peak. There are higher peaks all around, a waterfall booms ominously just beyond the garden fence, and the garden itself looks down a fanged and merciless valley which makes you think of solidified Fascism.

P.S. It has rained all day.

August 25th

We leave for Bergen this afternoon.

Henry has been reading guidebooks so intensely, since we left England, that his vocabulary is beginning to sprout little tendrils like "vertiginous heights" and "luxuriant vegetation." He told an English girl at breakfast this morning that Stockholm is a city of wide, clean streets and magnificent panoramas, and when I picked him up on it afterwards, he said it was all he could do to stop himself from adding,

"Many pleasant boating trips are available for the tourist."

ON BOARD THE *Jupiter*—It is brilliant weather, though with a heavy swell, and Henry and I have a cabin opening on deck. After lunch two ladies came and sat down outside our door. One of them kept saying solicitously to the other, "Do you mind the motion? Shall I get you some brandy? Do you feel queasy? Would you like a little lemon?" The other lady started out with the healthiest of denials, but they grew progressively fainter. Henry and I tried not to listen, but after a while we began to avoid each other's eyes. At this juncture, however, the man in the next cabin leaned out and said to the Angel of Mercy, "Please, lady, would you mind taking that damn propaganda somewhere else?"

The Angel made an explosive little sound, like the popping sigh when papers thrown on top of a blaze suddenly catch fire.

"*Come*, dear," she said to her victim, and they went away.

August 29th

CANTERBURY—England, and especially Canterbury, seems peaceful and natural after Norway, and Canterbury is by all odds my favorite

athedral. A narrow, medieval street called
Mercery Lane leads to a massive gate—a building in itself—whose carvings are so worn that
he gate is like a big mound of grey butter which
has begun to melt. Beyond the gate are lawn
and trees, with the Cathedral rearing up in
inewy solidity and looking exactly the way you
think a cathedral is going to look before you
have ever seen one.

Exeter is a baby cathedral; Ely is too big and
goes gangling on long after it ought to have
stopped; and it is hard to get a good look at
Westminster Abbey, because of the surrounding
buildings. I liked Salisbury best, with its single
central tower, until I saw Canterbury. But Canterbury has two western towers to balance its
central one, which makes you realize immediately that the design of Salisbury is the design
of a short-handled mop. However, I do not like
the interior of Canterbury as much as I do its
exterior. The Transitional choir may be, as the
guidebook energetically says it is, the finest
Transitional in England, but to my mind Transitional always looks as if a busy little man had
been locked up in a very tall wine cellar with
nothing to amuse him but some paste and a
basket of acanthus leaves.

One of the most agreeable things about Canterbury is that its history is so easily assimilable.
It is the kind of history which comes up and

takes you by the coat lapel—the door throug]
which both Becket and the assassins entered th
Cathedral, the spot where the Archbishop fel]
and the stone steps worn into hollows by knee]
ing pilgrims; not to mention the Black Princ
in golden effigy, with his gauntlets, helme
shield and jacket hanging above the tomb. Com
pared to Becket and the Black Prince, the mis
sionary bishops of Exeter and the Cambridge
college-founders interred at Ely are a mer
featureless rabble.

August 30t

This morning we took the bus to a lonely littl
village some miles northeast of Canterbur
called St. Nicholas at Wade. St. Nicholas a
Wade has a brown pub and brown thatche
roofs and a brown church said to date from th
year 1200. Unlike most of the English villages
have seen, it is not sheltered, even by trees, bu
stands in the midst of a wide sweep of whea
fields with nothing on the horizon except th
square towers of the Saxon church at Reculver
on the North Sea. I felt guilty about going or
and leaving it, so old and solitary and unpre
tending, all alone.

We walked across the fields from St. Nichola
to Birchington, on the coast. Kent is hilly as fa
as Canterbury, but near the sea the ground
flattens into mere loops and swirls. When the

path dipped into hollows, all that could be seen was grain and sky, and even on the crests there was only a line of woods ahead and the twin towers of Reculver over our shoulders. It is the roomiest landscape I have seen in England. We stopped at Birchington—a neat, dull town—for lunch and then walked to Margate to catch the bus back to Canterbury. The walk to Margate was along chalk cliffs above the sea, but it led into an increasingly thicker miasma of those Greco-like buildings the late Victorians were fond of putting up at summer resorts. Margate they say, has the finest air in England. In reality, it has the only air in England. The rest of the country has to get along the best it can with an alien compound which shuffles into the nostrils like disinherited soup.

The English always speak of Margate as a place of vulgar and feverish gaiety, but the beach and promenade, at least, look to an American like a Quaker meeting. The sun is weak and the English are modest, so there is hardly any more flesh on view than there is in Piccadilly Circus. The bathers do not run races or play ball or stand on their hands or carry on conversations with friends a quarter of a mile away. Instead, they knit or hold hands or merely sit and stare out to sea. On the promenade grass, a few solemn individuals throw cricket balls with an overhand gesture which reminds

the startled foreigner of a ten-year-old girl re
signing from the neighborhood baseball team
in a towering huff. The pagan abandon of Mar
gate could be scraped together and piled up
under a thimble, but the visitors look as if it
would be a positive pleasure to go home on a
crowded subway with them at the end of the
day.

August 31s

Current lodging, a sixteenth-century house
which lines up approximately as follows:

Credits—Tiny, naive bedroom whose white
plaster walls, with wavy black uprights in
them, chuckle at night as if they were being
tickled when the firelight races over them

Diamond-paned windows looking out on
a Sleeping Beauty courtyard, formed by
gabled almshouses, where doubled-up old
men totter slowly back and forth among
the zooming flowers.

Pleasant novelty of having something
ancient and historic mixed in with com-
monplaces like combing hair, cleaning nails
and untying knots in shoestrings.

Debits—Floors which decide arbitrarily to go
down a step, so that the unwary guest lands
with a jar that strikes sparks from his spine.

144

Beams smudged with the scalps of tall people, including Henry's and mine.

Bathroom in the cellar—a long, prison-like room, windowless, with a terrified toilet crouching at one end and a spent and beaten bathtub flung into a clump of impenetrable shadows at the other. Visitors jump at seeing a towel on the floor, thinking it is whitened bones.

We have had very little rain since we came back from Norway, but the days are cool and the nights cold. The manageress (manager *Ess*, the English always pronounce it) of the Guest House has gotten used to our having a fire in the evening, though the first time Henry approached her on the subject, she started back as if he had asked her for a brace of concubines.

"But it's summer!" she exclaimed.

"That," said Henry gently, "is a matter of opinion."

The manager *Ess* is disturbing. Not having been able to decide whether running a Guest House makes her a lady or a non-lady, she alternates between being loftily genteel and pliantly humble, watching us sharply, meanwhile, to see what we will do. As we do not do anything, her manner towards us grows more and more marked by an angry perplexity. A good, round snub would settle her problem, and I imagine

she would rather have it settled downward than
not settled at all, but a good, round snub is a
hard thing to manage in cold blood. I do not
know what opposite gesture would convince her
that Henry and I regard her as a lady. Henry
suggests we say to her carelessly some afternoon,
"Would you like to join us? We're just going out
to put a few people in their places."

SANDWICH—The bus from Canterbury to
Sandwich takes less than an hour, but it goes
from inland into coastal landscape. We have a
balcony, and from it the sea is visible, two miles
away. Nearer at hand is smooth, green country
flattened down by air and sky and only occasionally interrupted by clumps of brawnily sensual English trees. Henry and I seem to be
almost the only occupants of the hotel, which is
large and not ungracious and which we like
very much. Our dining room waiter, a man
filled with headlong friendliness, tells us in por-
tentous accents that it is very quiet here in the
winter time. If it is any quieter than it is now
the management ought to charge admission just
for letting people come in and listen to it.

Sandwich has a "Millionaires' Corner" at
Sandwich Bay and a golf course described as the
146

t. Andrews of England, and it is expensive.
The town itself is small and flawlessly pictur-
sque, with narrow, crooked streets and houses
—humorously askew—which have had their
hair combed and their ears washed for the bene-
it of old ladies likely to be interested in lunch,
tmosphere and hand-woven woolens. The self-
onsciousness of Sandwich brings Stratford to
mind, but where Stratford offers itself to the
ourists like a promiscuous wench with no front
o her dress at all, Sandwich prefers to seduce
hem in a costly, come-on-boys-take-a-peek
rassière.

Nevertheless, it is a beautiful and tranquil
place, and there are streets and corners in the
own so full of a small, brown ripeness that you
vant to sink your teeth into them. An old barbi-
an at one of the town gates looks, in spite of its
owering and defiant name, as if it had been
aken out of a children's playroom. Two fat,
riendly little towers are joined by a connecting
tructure in between. The lower half of each
ower is black and white check, the upper half
built of reddish-brown wood, and the roofs
re red tile. The *tout ensemble* could hardly be
elied upon to frighten off a mouse.

September 6th

EXETER—We are here for a week while Henry
lans courses and attends committee meetings,

and then we go to Cornwall for a week or tw
until the college opens and we move into th
house at Yeobridge. We are staying at a hote
for this visit to Exeter, and a dispiriting estab
lishment it is—dark and cold and melanchol
and with the corners of its mouth turned down
Whenever I walk into it, I feel like a box of salt
water taffy inadvisedly straying among funera
baked meats. The whole week is already fille
up with invitations, to which, I admit guiltily—
for they are intended well—I am not lookin;
forward very much.

September 7t

We have flushed, of all things, an Englishma:
who does not talk about the weather, and wh
should it have to be, of course, but the man wh
is sailing for America at the end of this week t
take Henry's place? He was away when we wer
at Exeter in June, but he came to the hotel fo
dinner last night and charmed Henry and m
in two minutes flat. His name is Mr. Primros
and he is a quiet little man, carelessly dressed
with wristbones and an Adam's apple whick
though small, are noticeably prominent. Hi
most striking quality is that he succeeds in com
bining a very English repose with a wholly un
English curiosity. But he would be an origina
in any country, for he is the sort of person wh
does not mind being disagreed with and he re

sorts neither to the American plan of heading off opposition by a hasty and defiant statement of his own attitude nor to the English plan of smothering it by toplofty implications that we gentlemen all think alike and the last one to come around to our point of view is a rotten egg.

Mr. Primrose charms me by talking to me as if I were a human being and not A Woman, and he charms both of us by laughing. I am not one to look down my nose at the placid cheerfulness of the English, several hundred billion carloads of which would improve my countrymen beyond recognition. But what makes a visiting American feel most helpless and lonely in England is, I think, neither the food nor the climate nor the damp houses nor the relentless subservience of the lower classes nor the spectacle of English gentlemen being conscientiously banal under the impression that it represents a magnificent discipline. What makes an American realize sinkingly that this, by God, is alien corn is the relative scarcity of laughter. You can get a kind of whinnying sound out of the well-bred English merely by saying that it is raining, and the English who are not well-bred have a superlative gift for catching the humor of a situation. But when it comes to humorous language, American similes and metaphors land with a morbid thump in the midst of a puzzled silence. The only way to make the English laugh, as laughter

is understood in the United States, is to jab
them with your elbow and say out of the corner
of your mouth, "That's funny." Then they all
look nervously around at each other and allow
you two decibels of politely acquiescent mirth.

September 8th

Henry is busy, and I have been going dutifully about, either with or without him, to
lunches and teas and dinners. It is not especially
stimulating, and I am glad I will be eight miles
away in Yeobridge this winter. At the moment
I feel, with my invitations, like a shopper whose
arms are breaking under a load of packages
which will not be any fun to open on getting
home. A small college, I begin to suspect, is a
small college the world over. The one in Exeter
is more subdued and serious and less silly than
American institutions customarily are. The students are better mannered and less flauntingly
adolescent and all the activities connected with
the establishment are pursued with a great deal
of dignity. There are no fraternities, and ath-
letics are purely for exercise. But the faculty has
the same proportion of people who think they
are too good for their jobs, the same handful
who actually are too good and do not think so,
and the same round of liturgical entertainments
with which the professors and their wives fight
off the consciousness of mediocrity.

What gives faculty entertainments in Exeter a slightly unfamiliar cast is the Double Standard of English conversation. Men who talk well and intelligently to Henry at meetings and committees wag a mischievous finger at me and say archly, "You women! I know you!" (The instinct to reply, "Chrissake, kid, you got me wrong" all but chokes me.) Englishmen, from what I can see, do not talk to women if they can possibly avoid it, and if they must talk to them, they keep the conversation inexorably down to their idea of the level of feminine understanding. And Englishwomen—even the brainy ones, apparently—meekly concur. Brought up in girls' schools and trained to be as much as possible like perambulating salads, they are incurably afraid of men. Whatever the rest of the world thinks of the English gentleman, the English lady regards him apprehensively as something between God and a goat, and equally formidable on both scores.

September 9th

Mr. Primrose is handsomely allowing us to use his car while he is away. Not that the car itself is particularly handsome. English cars, after American, seem feeble and unprepossessing, both of which qualities Mr. Primrose's machine has to a degree. If an old suit of armor were pounded into the right shape and provided, more or less as an afterthought, with four cylinders, the result would be indistinguishable from Mr. Primrose's little barouche. Henry, once he gets his knees under the dashboard, cannot get them out again to step on the starter and has to press it down with his fingers. But he closed with Mr. Primrose's offer thankfully, because with a car he will be more or less independent of the buses in going to and from Exeter. Mr. Primrose himself is not vainglorious about the vehicle. "Twelve and a half horse power," he said, pointing to the hood, and added thoughtfully, "Rocking horses."

September 10th

I went out to Yeobridge today to see Mrs. Turney about the final arrangements. Her house, after the hotel, looked so bright and human that it took a strong effort of will for me to tear myself away. Mrs. Turney says I must learn to call the living room the drawing room, for in England a living room, if the term is used at all, means the kind of apartment where you put all the old, broken-down furniture and give the dogs and the children a free hand.

September 11th

Mr. Primrose sailed today, which gave both Henry and me a definite sense of loss. I have begun to realize, since I have been here, what a tough, ungracious place New York must seem to anyone accustomed to English life. But Mr. Primrose is one of the most essentially unfrightenable people I have ever met, so I am not alarmed for him.

September 13th

PLYMOUTH—Last night was one of the occasions when travel seems worth its weight in labor pains. We left Exeter late in the afternoon, drove across Devonshire, and arrived in Plymouth after dark and in the rain. It was our idea to locate the center of town and look for a hotel, but the center of Plymouth showed slightly less inclination to be located than the Holy Grail. We rode for miles along wet car tracks which swerved and looped in graceful abandon and ultimately led with a great flourish into other car tracks. Directions from passers-by, though cheerful, set what must be a new standard of futility.

"You know where the clock is," begins the passer-by masterfully.

"No," replies Henry.

A grieved, this-is-not-in-my-department look comes over the face of our informant. But he rallies and starts to outline a plan for getting to the clock. Those plans for getting to the clock took me back to the days when I was in college and had, or thought I had, to listen with interest and sympathy to explanations of the five-man lateral pass. At long last we found a police-man who said there was a hotel just down the street. By that time it did not even occur to us to ask what kind of hotel it was.

You could not say whether the hostelry was clean or not, it was too dimly lit, but it was the sort of place where you hesitated to grasp any-thing very firmly. Our bedroom had an iron bedstead, a mattress with a ski jump in the mid-dle of it, and the inevitable pink silk draperies. We left the suitcases and went out to eat, as—if the smell in the corridors was any indication—it was Human Sacrifice Night at the hotel. Three-quarters of an hour of walking failed to disclose a restaurant which was still open. Just as I was saying tragically that we would have to go back to the room and eat toothpaste, Henry noticed a place of decidedly humble aspect which seemed in two minds about closing up. We hurried in, and an absent-minded waitress gave us a pot of tea, supplemented after fifteen minutes by a piece of steak which had evidently been put to bed for the night and resented being disturbed.

Dinner, if you could call it that, concluded, I took a deep breath and said, "Anyway, let's have a drink." But it was "after hours"; Eng-land, with sublime disregard for the needs of sensitive foreigners, had settled down into her

154

nightly purity; and there was nothing to do but return uncheered to the hotel and go gingerly to bed.

CAWSAND (CORNWALL)—We left Plymouth as soon as possible, having a grudge against it, and crossed the Sound to Cornwall. The original plan was for us to spend the rest of the time before October first, when we move into Mrs. Turney's house, proceeding at leisure down the coast of Cornwall. But Mr. Primrose's car, which had all it could do to drag the pageant of its bleeding heart across the hills of Devon, lost consciousness completely when confronted with the hills of Cornwall. We had to lift it to the sofa and unfasten its stays. When this debacle occurred, we were in a little village called Cawsand, just across the Sound from Plymouth, and Cawsand being decidedly appetizing of aspect, we decided to stay here for a while.

Cawsand has less patience and sweetness about it and more severity and guts than English villages seem customarily to have. It stands on a hilly little peninsula which, having Plymouth Sound on one side and the Atlantic Ocean on the other two, is instinct with horizons. Cawsand itself has been boldly tacked to the side of a steep descent which plunges suicidally into Plymouth Sound. The streets of the village are virtually perpendicular, and are rendered still more improbable by being in addition so narrow that a four-year-old child with a pail in its hand constitutes a traffic jam. Sprinkled in among the white cottages are others which have been plastered in burnt orange or salmon pink or tan, departures from the norm which give the village a remarkable air of independence. Along some of the streets, a sea wall with purple-flowering vines growing over it interposes benevolently to keep you from falling over on to the dark, malign coastal rocks below.

Though a shelter of woods flanks Cawsand on either side, tall, green hills rise baldly up in back of it. These, combined with the stretched-out pieces of water, make the houses, which in other English villages seem to be rubbing up against each other like puppies in a basket, seem in Cawsand to be huddling together for the definite purpose of protection. This blue-browed and rock-ribbed Cornish austerity makes a pleasant change after the lushness of Devon. I think we will stay here until the long-awaited first of October.

September 17th

The English hotels we have stayed in so far always seemed to me expressly planned to dis-

ourage people from remaining away from
home overnight. The red plush. The black wal-
nut. The framed engravings of lovers' quarrels.
The Pampas grass. The fireplaces blocked up
with nasty little brutes of gas heaters. Whenever
we checked out of a hotel this summer, it was
with the moral certainty that the manager immediately retired to his office for a few minutes
of private rejoicing. "There," he would say,
looking out of the window after us, "that'll
teach 'em to go gadding about!"

But the hotel we are staying at in Cawsand
has wide, light staircases with brown oak chests
on the landings. Set on the hill above the village,
it is a big, rambling stone house, formerly a
private residence. We have been given a large
room with a southern exposure and tall casement windows. There is a white mantel over a
bona fide fireplace, a four-poster bed with a
faded canopy, and a cushioned window seat
where you can sit and look out over the roofs of
the village to the liners standing sedately in the
Sound and being milked by tenders. The place
would be perfect, except for the food, which is
the worst yet. There is no chance of digesting it,
because it tears the bottom right out of your
stomach first.

September 19th

The owner of the hotel, a retired naval officer,
has just been up to the room and built us a hand-

some fire. He is a strong-and-silenter. He build
fires and worms dogs and whittles out boats and
evens off tennis courts, performing these and
similar offices with an air of manifest enjoy
ment, and he never wastes a word—largely, I
suppose, because he does not have to. His
shrewd, weather-beaten face is a conversation in
itself. Two of his sons are in the navy, and two
more are still at the stage of leaving spare miz-
zenmasts and strings of dead fish on the drawing
room chairs, a habit which adds perceptibly to
the informality of the atmosphere. The two sons
appear briefly, dry, in the morning and re-
appear briefly, dripping sea water, at six in the
evening. They have beautiful manners, which
maintain a sort of warring equilibrium with a
strong conviction that people who cannot sail
boats ought not to be allowed to waste the time
of people who can.

September 21st

Mr. Primrose's car is able to get about a little
again, and yesterday we ventured to drive down
the coast as far as a little place called Mega-
vissey. It was a beautiful drive, all cliffs and
clouds and rainbows and dark rocks and wide
blue stretches of sea, though, as Henry pointed
out, when you try to put it in words you only
sound as if you were describing a black eye. I
had thought Cawsand precipitate, but we saw

ther villages which were considerably more so.
t feels as if one were either reading or dream-
ng, to look at those rugged and colorful Cornish
illages, stepping down brusque hillsides into
heir Morte d'Arthur coves. But the inhabitants,
Henry's colleagues in Exeter say, are so inbred
hat in some places fifty per cent of the school-
children are either morons or nearly so. Hand-
ome is that handsome does.

September 22nd

I went into one of the crowded, stuffy little
hops of Cawsand today—it was not much
arger than a good-sized dog kennel—to get
ome oranges with which to outflank the hotel
carbohydrates. By borrowing from the neighbors, the shop managed to get together a dozen
oranges, but they were hardly bigger than wal-
nuts and when cut into, proved to be filled with
a vegetable equivalent of absorbent cotton.
However, we are having a full moon, and this
andscape by moonlight is so beautiful that
Henry and I, going for our nightly walk, almost
have to bring each other home in pails.

One of the pleasantest things about coming to
England is the number of hitherto skipped-over
ittle phrases which suddenly take on meaning.
"Draw the curtains," for instance. The English,
nstead of window shades like ours, have heavy
curtains at the windows which are pushed aside

during the daytime and drawn together at night. In this hotel, though, there are no curtains at all, and we go to sleep at night in a beatific combination of moonlight and firelight. I go to sleep, that is. Henry explains sombrely that it keeps him awake. Of all Henry's beliefs perhaps his favorite one is that he cannot fall asleep if there is so much as a pinprick of light or a hair-scrape of noise in the room. Actually he drowses in boiler factories and nods off under klieg lights, but he gets so much simple pleasure out of being resigned to an insomnia he does not have, that I have abandoned the heartless statistics of the situation and given the legend its innocent head.

September 25th

Henry has gone up to Exeter for the opening of the college, but I am staying on in Cawsand until the first of the month.

September 29th

Tomorrow we move into Yeobridge, and from now on there will be a whole house to spread out in and I shall wear ironed underwear again. Whee!

PART III

Yeobridge

The day started rainy, but by the time we reached Yeobridge this afternoon, the house and garden were floating on sunlight and looking so snug and pretty and delectable that I said I guessed I would not bother with going back to the womb. I nearly changed my mind, though, when we had had tea and I had to begin unpacking. Stuffing my own rudimentary wardrobe into the nearest drawer is a matter of five minutes, but Henry has a sense of property like Silas Marner and Andrew Mellon combined. You could probably (if he were not so thin) take a pound of flesh from Henry without encountering any more opposition than an absent-minded "Ouch!", but try to separate him from his high school chemistry notes or the scarf his sister made for him when she was eight years old, and you find yourself up against something.

He not only cherishes, but he has brought to Europe with him, such objects as a topographical felt hat, bought in the Tyrol by some distant relative and passed around the family like a hot potato—until it got to Henry. He has brought to Yeobridge with him eight black dinner ties, every one of which has apparently seen years of service on the town gibbet. He has brought two tuxedos, both so old-fashioned that he looks like a heron in them and people stand still so as

not to frighten him away. When I was packing
the trunks in New York, I made one last heroic
effort to wean him, but he gave me a look of
such silent agony and reproach, even at the
compromise proposal to leave the things behind
in storage, that I was not proof against it.

Phyllis, however, did most of the unpacking.
When we first arrived, she was so frightened of us
that I thought she was going to cry, but I sent
her around to the post office to buy some stamps
and regain her composure, and by the time she
returned, her natural instinct for running things
had come irresistibly to the surface. She weeded
out Henry's sartorial driftwood and silently
stowed it in the attic; she whisked away part of
Mrs. Turney's dark-green and dark-brown library and Mydaughter's French and German
grammars to make room for the books we had
brought; she catechized me delicately on my
ideas about housekeeping and appeared surprised and relieved to discover that I am innocent of any. Finally, after a suitable interim, she
produced a dinner with magnificent roast beef
and an omelet so light that we had to lay our
knives across it and even then it struggled. We
haled her in and complimented her fervently on
the meal, which made her blush and look
pleased, but also a little startled, as if she were
not used to praise. It looks as if we have a para-
gon on our hands.

Henry's sartorial driftwood

Phyllis calls me "Adam." I got Henry to listen too, thinking I might be imagining, but there is no mistaking it. Not a trace of an initial "m." "Madame Bede" and "Adam Bovary" have been going through my head all day.

After a summer so wet and cold that I thought I was going to grow a coating of moss on the north side, the autumn has brought us a long spell, now, of decent weather. Decent, that is, in the English sense of not having more than one or two showers a day. I have spent the last two days walking in the deep, comfortable lanes which lead out of Yeobridge. One of the first things I like to know about a country town is where the roads go. ("Why not ask?" Henry would say.) Yeobridge lies about a mile back of the main road leading from Exeter up to North Devon, and the lanes of Yeobridge do not go anywhere. They merely lead into other lanes, which apparently continue slanting up hills and hopping off into valleys almost indefinitely. There are steep banks, six to ten feet high, on either side of the lanes, with hedgerows on top of the banks. You cannot see the fields above you, but sometimes you can hear the meditative footfalls and meek, slow-straining sound of harness where a team is ploughing. Here and there a little driveway leads up to the gate of a meadow, and on high ground you can climb up on the gate and see the countryside falling away below, misty and rich and so delicate it looks as if it would bruise if you stepped on it. The leaves are still green, and there is no sign of autumn.

October 4th

I cannot summon sufficient moral courage to tell Phyllis point-blank that I want to dispense with Mrs. Turney's ornaments. I have an intuition she will not approve. So I am stealthily putting them away a few at a time, hoping that the desecration, dawning gradually, will come as less of a shock. Today I secreted four cut glass bowls; several hymnals bound in mother-of-pearl; and a garnet brooch of a size to render any moderately fragile woman practically powerless. Phyllis has apparently not noticed.

October 5th

I paid my first visit to the Yeobridge post office today. It stands in the village square and looks so agreeable, with its thatched roof and crooked door and casement windows, that when you see it from the outside, you want to take it up in your lap and pet it. The inside, however, hardly lives up to the promise of the exterior. Going in the door, you find yourself in a room

166

about eight feet square with a threateningly low ceiling and only so much light as can wrestle its way in through a window not much larger than a handkerchief. The room is divided in half by a counter. On the customers' side a small doorway, crookedly curtained with a draggled cretonne, leads into the back room. On the postmistress' side an infinitesimal fireplace holds a grate which could not possibly accommodate more than a quart of coal. When I was there, a blackened pot perched on top of the fire was systematically giving off one of the evilest smells I have ever encountered. The rest of the postmistress' side is taken up with a rickety table, a broken chair and a collection of shelves, the shelves proceeding across the wall at a carefree slant and retaining apparently by sheer mesmerism an ancestral collection of garden tools, ink, twine, calendars, chocolate bars and small Union Jacks.

The postmistress herself is a broad-shouldered, sibylline woman with old-fashioned, silver-rimmed spectacles and a wide, grey, hairy face. My object in going to the post office was to explain that I use my maiden name in New York and that I might be receiving letters under it here. When I came in, the postmistress gave me a thoroughgoing smile and pointing to the watery daylight in the square outside, said, "'E bain't coom out yet, bain't 'er."

By a quick calculation, I decided that she must mean the sun.

"No," I said lightly, "but it'll be out this afternoon."

From the blind, seeking look that came over her face, I realized I had deafness to cope with, as well as dialect. Slowly and carefully, I embarked on my explanation, speaking with great distinctness and pausing between each word, but she merely looked at me in good-natured bewilderment. I began again. In the middle of the second attempt, she suddenly reared back and glared. I paused.

"Bain't 'ee morrit?" she asked thunderously.

"Married?" I replied. "Yes, yes, yes!" and nodded my head violently.

Her countenance cleared, and then dropped back into its smiling uncomprehension. I made one further attempt. At its conclusion, the postmistress put both hands on the edge of the counter, tipped her head back, and regarded me benignly.

"Chocolate?" she inquired.

"Never mind," I answered. "I'll send Phyllis over."

She caught the name immediately.

"Phyllis?"

"Phyllis," I replied loudly and reassuringly, backing toward the door. I gave her a large, bright, empty smile and with one last, clarion iteration of "Phyllis," I made my escape.

October 6th

The farmhouses in this region appear to be whited sepulchres. To see them standing in their soundless green valleys (the English are no great hands for hilltops) with their thatched roofs and thick, muscular-looking walls, with blanketing orchards behind and prodigious, tangled masses of flowers in front, you would think nothing in the world could be so serene and beautiful and gracious. But the interiors, what can be descried of them from a discreet stare while passing by, look dark and cramped and dirty. Phyllis, who speaks with indulgent scorn of "the country people," tells me the farmhouses are damp as sponges and that their inmates live mostly on black tea and piecrust. The farmers I have seen in the lanes—leisurely herding sheep or cows along in front of them, or riding ineffably deliberate plough horses, or driving two-wheeled carts at a pace which it would be exaggeration to call measured—are stained from head to foot with the red-brown Devon earth. They always greet me. If it is raining, they say, "Darty, uh?" in an approving tone of voice, as if they were commending me for being out in the wet, but if the sun is out, they only nod and smile.

The days melt away like cough drops on the tongue. I brush my hair and take a long walk and type out Henry's notes and stand for a while in the garden composing my face to look like a Landed Gent, and ping! the day is gone. The Devonshire countryside grows upon me like an obsession; I sometimes suspect that somebody has given me a philtre. Living in England, provincial England, must be like being married to a stupid but exquisitely beautiful wife. Whenever you have definitely made up your mind to send her to a home for morons, she turns her heart-stopping profile and you are unstrung and victimized again. The garden still spurts roses and snapdragons and Michaelmas daisies, which I cut and arrange at great length in bowls and vases. This pursuit I estimate to be about the sheerest waste of time I have ever indulged in. The flowers wilt and only have to be done all over again. Henry, being a native New Yorker, looks pained if his attention is called to flowers. And the flowers in the garden are virtually forcing the house right off the property as it is, without my introducing them into the drawing room to bore from within. But it is principally because it is so fruitless that I like to do it. It makes every day feel like Saturday afternoon.

I read a great deal, which takes more time here than it does at home, owing to the necessity for shifting every five minutes either nearer the fire or further away from it. At the end of half an hour, my chair is usually completely immobile, being hopelessly knotted up in the hearth rug, and I have to climb out and set things to rights again. And there is the additional necessity of poking the blaze four or five times an hour. I am a little bewildered, as a matter of fact, at the amount of titivation required by even the most promising-looking fire. But I perform all these offices tranquilly and even absent-mindedly, for the soft, moist, enervating air of Devon has the effect of taking the sting out of orneriness. In fact, I think the reason time goes so fast in Yeobridge and has such a lovely emollient quality is largely the climate. After half an hour of Devonshire air, your nerves are so relaxed they drag on the ground and you trip over them.

October 8th

While Phyllis was upstairs making the beds this morning, I smuggled three raffia wastebaskets into the closet under the stairs, also a life-sized portrait in stand-up frame of the great crested woodpecker and a selection of the lumpier and bulgier vases. The resulting gaps seem to me distinctly noticeable, but they still do not appear to have caught Phyllis's eye.

I have had two callers, a Mrs. Wadhams, who is young, and a Mrs. Pennard, who is not. Mrs. Wadhams, coming yesterday, caught me completely unawares. I remember that when I was a child, my mother had a calling card case which was kept in a box with the long white gloves she wore at her wedding, but if she ever used it, I have no recollection thereof. I myself have never paid a call in my life. (Where my acquaintances come from, I cannot tell. Somebody hangs them, all beribboned, on the doorknob of a May Day morning, and then runs quickly away.) At any rate, when Phyllis showed Mrs. Wadhams in, I was reading with both legs over the arm of the chair and my hair in a state which would have been very tempting to a broody hen. Mrs. Wadhams, fortunately, was disposed to be cheerful and informal and she did not seem to mind. She has a stocky, unimaginative body and a face which looks ten years too young for it. Her hair is golden as the traditional guinea and her complexion makes me feel like the beach at low tide. She is, I suppose, that "simple English girl" to whom the British are fond of referring with a tender and rather horticultural pride, as if they grew them on south walls, like apricots.

Mrs. Wadhams and I had twenty minutes of swift and sunny chatter, though it took me the first five to figure out what she had come for. The Wadhamses live in the house nearest ours, and Captain Wadhams is an officer in the Yeomanry, which seems to be a kind of militia officered by professional army men. They have a year-old son, and Mrs. Wadhams creates a distinct impression that he comes in a bad third in her affections, the pursuits of hunting and gardening easily nosing him out. In searching around for something to say, I asked her what schools there were in Yeobridge. She seemed surprised at the question, though she answered agreeably enough that the girls go to a Church of England school, which is where Phyllis went, and the boys to a grammar school. The gentry send their children away to school, only in Yeobridge the gentry's children (except for young Wadhams) are all grown up. She uses the word "gentry" with entire naturalness, and not as if she hoped I would notice it or as if she noticed it herself, but the expression bounced into me as if it had come from a slingshot.

When Mrs. Pennard called today, I was more or less prepared for her—which was a good thing, as Mrs. Pennard is no more disposed to be cheerful and informal than I am to take the veil. "A lettuce woman," I thought glibly when she came into the room, for she had grey hair and she wore a beautifully tailored grey tweed coat. But I gaped with surprise when I heard her voice. It has the teary whine of a slattern trying to put off the rent-collector. I found it hard to realize that she was speaking correct English. Looking with sudden attention at her face, I noticed that every line in it goes downward. It is a face that seriously undermines the repose of the beholder, for it keeps him hearkening willy-nilly for the soft, slow splash that will be Mrs. Pennard's countenance sliding down and landing sadly on Mrs. Pennard's bosom.

Mrs. Wadhams had told me that Mrs. Pennard would probably call. "She's the Big Five in Yeobridge," said Mrs. Wadhams in her light, schoolgirlish way. When Mrs. Pennard had gone and Phyllis brought the tea in, I asked, "Who is Mrs. Pennard, Phyllis? One of the local dowagers?" Poor Phyllis tries loyally to be the well-trained English servant, complete with poker face and Simonized (at least, in the presence of her betters) mind. But she is young, and the human being in her is so near the surface that it comes popping out like a jack-in-the-box at the lightest stimulus. When I mentioned Mrs. Pennard, her round, clean young features fell into an expression which was the best she could get out of them in the way of weary distaste.

Mrs. Pennard, it appears, was widowed a good many years ago by a hunting accident and has devoted her time ever since to charity. The list of her good works sounds like freight-car loadings in a banner year and they must cost her considerable amounts in time, trouble and money. She visits the well-to-do and gets their support for the Nursing Association. She visits the poor and. . . . Here Phyllis let her sentence trail off. She tramps through miles of muddy lanes in bad weather to visit bedridden old women on outlying farms who never have any other callers. And, from Phyllis's somewhat elliptical account, she regards the manners and morals of servant girls as having been especially committed to her supervision by a Deity who had given them up in despair Himself.

Poor Mrs. Pennard! I suppose she owes her weeping-willow face and voice to the mournful discovery that crowbar charity is the least rewarding of human pastimes. But one would certainly never suspect that that simulacrum of Niobe concealed a *force majeure*, and I do not see how she contrives to keep her subjects in order —unless it is that everyone is hopelessly cowed by the goodness of her intentions.

October 10th

We have inherited a gardener from Mrs. Turney, a big man in stained brown clothes who comes once a week. He speaks the Devonshire dialect, rendered even broader and softer by the fact that he has no teeth. When he talks, he sounds like a bland diet. The incomprehension appears to be mutual, however, because after his first day here, he went around to the kitchen door and asked Phyllis if that was English Henry and I were using.

October 11th

Henry came home early today and was in time to have tea with me. It was raining, but gently and rather apologetically, and the sheep were bleating on the hills beyond the orchard. I had built the fire up into a tidy little inferno and we had raspberry jam and an unfamiliar toasted article, sweet and feathery and very good, called a Sally Lunn. Henry says his English students are politer, more serious and much better grounded than his fledglings in New York, and they take notes with flattering alacrity. They are, in fact, putty in his hands— except when it comes to talking. Apparently they have all been imbued with the idea that students should be seen and not heard, and they see no reason for abandoning this policy merely on the representations of some fly-by-night academe from America. If there should be a tiny spurt of class discussion, only the men participate. The women sit rigid and tongue-

ied. But evidently it is six of one and half a
dozen of the other. His American students, according to Henry, are bold and lively and ar-
ticulate—to the point of effrontery—in using
what specks and fragments of knowledge they
have, but their intellectual background, or lack
of it, has Henry starting from his sleep with
hollow groans. And they coolly refrain from
lifting a finger to improve it.

Both Mrs. Wadhams and Mrs. Pennard,
when they called, spoke of the college in Exeter
with pitying condescension. Mrs. Pennard said
tremulously that she understood you did not
get a very good class of people there, and Mrs.
Wadhams—referring, no doubt, to the sprin-
kling of Egyptian and Syrian students at the
college—remarked cheerfully that she did not
know it was for white people, she thought it was
only for blacks. The Wadhams-Pennard attitude arises, I think, from the fact that most of
the students are poor and are trying to pull
themselves up a class or two by getting an
education.

The English have refined upon our naive
American way of judging people by how much
money they happen to have at the moment. The
subtler English criterion is how much expensive, upper-class education they have been able
to afford. Consequently, in England, having

had money (provided it was not too mushroomy a phase) is just as acceptable as having it, since the upper-class mannerisms persist, even after the bankroll has disappeared. But never having had money is unforgivable, and can only be properly atoned for by never trying to get any. This arrangement is responsible for certain sniffs and snobbish inflections which bring an American to his feet with hackles rising, but it has nevertheless one felicitous result. The modest-income people, not having been pelted with success stories, settle cheerfully down to make their terms with life on whatever scale it happens to present itself, which gives the whole country, apparently, a refreshing freedom from our common complaint of bootstrap hysteria.

October 13th

We are having an Indian summer, though they call it Michaelmas summer over here. A plain grey sky covers up the morning, but in the afternoons the sun comes out and flows lemonishly over the landscape. I wonder, now, that I could ever have read Keats' *Ode to Autumn* without noticing that it celebrates an entirely different season from the American autumn. The year expires placidly in Devonshire, like a saintly clergyman unobtrusively breathing his last during an after-dinner nap. There are no purple asters or goldenrod, no shameless blue skies, no maples to give a bright, consumptive sparkle to the woods. The tang and challenge and triumphal grapiness of the American season are completely absent here, where the cool air comes up wetly against the cheek, even when the sun is out. Though the trees are beginning to turn yellow and brown and the woods look like English tweeds, the grass stays green. Phyllis says it keeps green all winter. The quality of the autumn is silvery and unbreathing and otherworldly, and there is lavender in everything— at the horizon, in the clouds and on the hills, as as well as among the chrysanthemums which boil up impartially in the gentry's gardens and around the thatched cottages and mean, redbrick houses where the ungentry live.

October 14th

Availing myself of Phyllis's afternoon out, I put away several large basketfuls of ornaments today. It is now possible to breathe out fairly heavily in the drawing room without hearing anything fall over. I still have four clocks and a selection of fans to go, however. The pictures I am leaving for Henry to weed out. I know nothing whatsoever about pictures and cannot even tell whether they are hanging right side out except by looking at the frames.

CALLERS

Mrs. Hayes—Small, sharp-eyed woman who looks as if she had been hung up on a rafter to dry, like bacon. Has large place & sells apples, chickens & eggs. Says Mrs. Turney buys from her & indicated, with great cheerfulness but unmistakable determination, that she intends me to buy too. Dawning antagonism in me apparently not noticed by Mrs. Hayes. Usual conversation: English weather, English scenery. Saying good-bye, Mrs. H. tells me that really she would never have taken me for an American. Reply impulsively that it doesn't show when I have my clothes on, but she ought to see my back. Mrs. Hayes thinks a moment & then laughs. Hayes laugh gives me the shivers. It comes at one-minute intervals & sounds exactly like egg-beater.

Mr. & Mrs. Vinnicombe—Vinnicombes, according to Wadhams, "keen on music." Tall, timid old couple, he strikingly handsome under shock of white hair, she gaunt & silent & badly dressed, but lean brown face full of an idea of the quality of life. Vinnicombes ask hesitantly what America is actually like. "We only know from the films," they say. First down for the Vinnicombes.

Mr. and Mrs. V. devotees of string quartets.

Manniest man's man since Attila the Hun

This, for Henry, equivalent to finding gold in back yard. Henry has hopeless passion for string quartets, either home- or custom-made. When first married, suggested I should learn to play cello. Have spent best years of life assiduously snatching Henry from paths of speeding motors (an opportunity for service which occurs about twice daily), but cello proposition struck me as exceeding bounds of reason by several parallels of latitude. Henry dashed on learning Vinni-combes do not play. He brought violin & viola to Europe with him—& would not put them in hold on boat, though stateroom so crowded he had to stand them up in wash-basin. Vinni-combes, however, have only victrola in Yeo-bridge & we are invited to come & hear it.

General & Mrs. Burton—Asked Mr. Vinni-combe who pugnacious-looking gentleman in fur-bearing tweeds might be whom I encounter frequently hurling himself through lanes. "That old buck," said Mr. V. irreverently, "that's the General."

Complete mystery how soft-spoken little Mrs. Burton ever induced General to come with her when she called. General manniest man's man since Attila the Hun. Silent except for explosive & rather juicy hur-rumphs. Face softened, how-ever, when I said I go for walk every day, even in rain. Appeared to notice for first time that I was in room. I followed up advantage quickly by asking about hunting. General regarded me with what might almost be called attention.

General used to hunt five days a week. Forbidden now—heart condition. Makes it plain he regards heart conditions as concerted whimsies on part of entire medical profession. Threnody on hunt in Midland Counties, scene of General's earlier triumphs. Terrain is flat in Midlands. Pack in Yeobridge, General tells me, but adds contemptuously the country so hilly that sport inconsequential. Burtons, nevertheless, always go to Yeobridge meets & watch them draw the first cover. Mrs. Burton invites me to go too, when season starts first of November. General looks startled. Mrs. B. hurries him off before he has opportunity to ask her what she did that for. When Burtons have left, I realize I have forgotten to ask what drawing first cover means.

The Parson—"He's very intellectual. You'll like him" (Wadhams). Both statements untrue. Parson, like practically all of Yeobridge, silver-haired. Slow-spoken man, loaded to gunwales with false benignity. Has habit of selecting longest word in sentence & repeating it. Conversation turned on Mrs. Wadhams, whom Parson calls splendid young woman, splendid. Parson knows her family. They live in Kent. Parson refers to Kent as if it were curious, esoteric place at least thousand miles away. Have noticed English

182

fond of talking of England as if it were size of
North America.

"I know them well," intones Parson. Sombre
pause. "I buried the father."

I suppress inclination to ask what else you
could do with him.

"A brilliant cricketer. Brilliant," continues
Parson. He leans forward. "They always called
him Toddles."

"Toddles," I say automatically. Benevolent
smile from Parse.

Parse represents self as extremely glad to
have Americans in village. Homily on our two
great nations, delivered with Jovian affability
& kind of surprised pleasure, as if Parson had
only just discovered that U. S. an English-
speaking country. He takes leave in sunset blaze
of kindliness & avuncular jollity, which makes
me feel consummate hypocrite, for have done
nothing to earn Parse's esteem beyond sitting
still & letting him talk. Realize sadly that polite passivity commits one to good deal of hypoc-
risy, as other people see in you only what they
want to see, unless definitely notified to con-
trary.

Mrs. Northrup—Only female in Yeobridge an
American would consider well-dressed. Said by
Parse to be terribly, terribly clever because
three daughters are London doctors. Mrs.

Northrup, perhaps by reason of being Scotswoman, actually does stand out among other Yeobridge matrons. Does not mention either weather or scenery. Refers several times to difference in our respective ages, which makes me feel like girl reporter interviewing Academie Française, but is refreshing change from other Yeobridge gents & gentesses, who assume dismayingly that we are all sixty-five years old together. Mrs. Northrup & I talk about books we have been reading, but in spite of liveliest disposition to agree with each other, arrive at no very successful meeting of the minds, for Mrs. N. thinks Mark Twain's *Yankee* vulgar & believes G. K. Chesterton is more for men, really. I nevertheless find it remarkably piquant not to be discussing English climate.

Mrs. Northrup, when applied to, instructs me kindly in procedure of returning calls. Suppose information commonplace enough, but all new to me. Mrs. Northrup also anxious for Henry & me to visit paper factory, which is about 3 mi. away down valley. I like Mrs. Northrup & do not wish to be too skeptical, but cannot help thinking privately that factory must be tame & domesticated establishment, as Yeobridge gentry hate to be reminded England an industrial country.

"Of course, we're the most mechanized people in the *world*," they say hastily, "but"—more slowly, & smiling hypnotically right into your eye—"this is the real England, isn't it?"

Parse's Wife—Said by Mesdames Pennard, Wadhams & Vinnicombe to be well-dressed. From bearing & manner, obvious Wife thinks so too, though she is not patch on Mrs. Northrup. Wife has navy-blue hat, presentable but not inspired. Navy-blue dress no different from customary English shroud except in being pulled in scintilla tighter around waist. Would still require divining rod to find out if anyone in it. Orange chiffon scarf at neck; bright red purse; pink stockings; grey shoes trimmed with brown; brown gloves. If Parse's Wife well-dressed, I am Florence Nightingale.

Wife comes in smiling, breathing poise like garlic, but eyes so hard & antagonistic I can almost see dotted lines converging on me. Because H. & I have not been to church? But Mrs. Northrup says freely has not been to church in 20 years. Realize, at any rate, I am being punished, though Lord knows for what, possibly inexcusable impudence of being citizen of my native country, since Wife makes immediate attack on Americanism, as being my weakest point. Must be staggering change for me to come & live in England. Child of two could see she means change for better. I take firm grip on self & resolve not to be provoked out of politeness.

During subsequent conversation, Wife informs me, with series of blinding smiles:

1. Americans do not get enough exercise,
2. Skyscrapers are too dreadful,
3. Parse's Wife fears marriage a mockery in America,
4. It is only decent for America to help England in case of war.

At this last effrontery, am too angry for any speech at all, polite or otherwise. Parse's Wife, misunderstanding silence, apologizes prettily for talking about foreign affairs. Says she finds them so intensely interesting. I am stung to utterance.

"That's all right," I say generously. "You're not taking me out of my depth."

Wife goggles. Is literally slack-jawed. But jaws snap together next moment (not, unfortunately, closing on tongue) & goggle sunk without trace in meringue of charm. We part with amiability, rather tentative & uncertain on my part, but pure Decorated Gothic on Wife's.

October 16th

Phyllis has finally noticed the strip-tease act that has been going on with the ornaments. She looks mournfully at the bare tables, but says nothing.

186

The faculty at the college are divided about
half and half on the question of dressing for
dinner, but in Yeobridge we never abandon for
a moment the pretence that we are all living in
Warwick Castle. When Henry and I dined with
the Wadhamses last night, dressing was so thoroughly taken for granted that the subject was
not even mentioned. Captain Wadhams proved
to be a large, red-cheeked man with a sleek and
shining brown moustache. He looks as if he had
been made to order as a husband for Mrs. Wadhams, and, in a sense, I suppose he was. But
his curiosity about the Yankees (which is Yeobridge's name for Henry and me) is less artless
and child-like than his wife's. Though he
greeted us with great affability, there was a
sparkle of apprehension about him. Obviously
he regarded his guests as not untinctured with
dynamite and I suspect that left to himself, he
would not have asked us to dinner without trying us out first at something less sacred, like tea.

The Captain was faultlessly tailored, and
watching Henry—in his Old Ironsides dinner
clothes—shaking hands with our host, I felt the
pang of mingled pity and annoyance which
women experience when their lovers or husbands are appearing at a disadvantage. I hoped,
however (though it seemed unlikely), that the

Captain would have the same feeling about Mrs
Wadhams and me, for Mrs. Wadhams was tum-
bled into a pink taffeta which could have looked
no worse if someone had carelessly erected a
haymow on top of it and then forgotten about
it for a season or two.

We stood around the fire and drank sherry
and said My, what beautiful weather. From
English, we went to American weather, the attributes of which struck Mrs. Wadhams as extremely funny, though the Captain looked
dubious, as if not having English weather might
some day prove to be a very serious matter.
Suddenly somebody coughed at the door. The
Captain sprang forward and ushered in a tall,
gaunt old lady called Auntie. Auntie walked
with a cane and she wore a great many rings
and rustled when she moved, but her handshake ought not to be used except as a tourni-
quet. She asked us how we liked England. That
is to say, the English do not exactly "ask" how
you like England. They wave the question in
the air, as if it were a chiffon scarf—graceful but
hardly necessary. When Henry had politely set
at rest the curiosity which Auntie did not have,
we went in to dinner.

There was no fire in the dining room, and as
I entered and the chill, damp air struck my bare
arms, I came fairly close to asking Mrs. Wadhams if she has trouble with stalactites. The

188

dinner, though prosaic, was nevertheless better than I had expected. By the time we got to the entree, the Captain was feeling reassured about his Boeotian guests. His nervousness melted visibly and the conversation whipped gaily around the table like rags in a high wind. Mrs. Wadhams asked us what we did in America and Captain Wadhams told us. Auntie said she once knew some Americans in Italy and they were charming. The Captain, who was not listening, answered, "Quite." Henry made little jokes which I thought were better as protective coloration than as humor, but which enthralled the Wadhamses. As for me, I smiled and smiled and smiled unendingly and silently fortified myself by remembering that people do not die of goose flesh, however probable it sometimes seems.

After dinner I took a glass of port. The Captain offered it to me, but as soon as I took it I realized that Auntie and Mrs. Wadhams had declined and that not only Auntie's eyebrows, but her whole face, seemed about to be snatched up to heaven, like Elijah. Everybody waited for me to finish my wine, which I did in such a hurry that it ran down over my chin and the glass left a mark on the cloth when I set it down. But the Captain remarked paternally that no doubt I was unused to drinking wine. Henry's face would have given me away if anyone had thought to look at it, but no one did. Auntie

was reunited to her countenance and the tensio
eased immediately. We all got up and Henr
vacantly started to follow Mrs. Wadhams an
Auntie and me out of the room. I hung bac
until he bumped into me and then gave him a
infinitesimal push in the stomach. As a rule
Henry is no more conscious of secret message
from me at social gatherings than he is of ultra
violet rays when he sits on the beach, but thi
time, fortunately for the Captain's nerves, h
caught on and turned back.

Alone in the drawing room, Auntie and Mr:
Wadhams and I talked about the servant prob
lem. Or rather, Auntie talked and Mrs. Wad
hams laughed and I listened.

"That wretched Holcomb woman," sai
Auntie to Mrs. Wadhams, "has lunch an *hou*
earlier on Sundays so the maids can get out. I
makes my girls frantic," she added with humor
ous impatience. "They aren't out till half pa:
four."

"I suppose she has a cold meal, too," supple
mented Mrs. Wadhams whimsically, smilin
at me.

I smiled back uneasily, aware that it was prob
ably branded on my forehead in eighteen-poin
italics that I myself have lunch an hour earlie
on Phyllis's day out—aware also that there wa
probably a P. S. on the brand stating that las
winter Henry and I had dinner at six o'cloc.

vo nights a week so that our then maid could
ttend divine service at a Harlem church called
Pray For You, You Pray For Me.

The English treatment of servants, however—
nderpaying them, overworking them, "keep-
1g them in their places," and talking about
1em in a fashion that makes you surprised,
hen the maid comes into the room, to see that
1e has vertebrae—used to rouse in me more in-
ignation than it does now. The servants seem
) ask for it. Even Phyllis, who has emerged
om Mrs. Turney's training with a smaller than
rdinary king-slave complex, is horrified at my
leaning my own shoes and has to be soothed
ith tactful explanations of the virtuosity of
merican shoe shining. And this though Phyllis
on the job from six in the morning till ten at
ight, while I do nothing all day long but read
nd walk and keep a diary and occasionally
nd Henry a helping hand. Phyllis's friends,
om what I can gather, absolutely insist on be-
1g bullied and exploited. It proves (luscious
1ought!) that they are working for gentlefolk.

At this point in my meditations, Henry and
1e Captain returned and the conversation be-
ame what is known as general. That is to say,
1e Captain and Auntie talked about somebody
alled Cousin Francis, whose eccentricities they
ppeared to find highly diverting, while Mrs.
Vadhams obligingly gave Henry and me

snatches of explanation, so that we could laugh
too. This we obligingly did, albeit somewha
mirthlessly, because by the time we had gotten
the necessary background of an anecdote, the
point had about as much impetus as a G. A. R
veteran.

And then after a while we went home.

October 18th

CLEAN-UP DAY

1. It seems to me one of the principal difference
   in the feeling-tone of English and American
   life comes from the fact that Americans are
   prone to favor you with their opinions and
   to do it, moreover, in the manner of an office
   boy favoring letters with stamps at five min
   utes to five, whereas the English think of an
   opinion as something which a decent person
   if he has the misfortune to have one, does all
   he can to hide.

2. I sometimes wonder what living in Yeobridge
   would be like if we did not have Phyllis. In
   spite of her suppliant Yes-Adams and No
   Adams, she contrives to make the caller
   seem, in contrast, a collection of faded da
   guerreotypes. You can get your teeth into
   Phyllis, and unless I am greatly mistaken
   she can be trusted to return the compliment

3. Two things I have not seen in England: (a) people working at enjoying themselves and (b) people enjoying themselves. Every schoolboy knows that Americans do not enjoy themselves. But they do have a concept of enjoyment and, indeed, put themselves through a whole variety of tortures in its name. In England, on the other hand, there appears to be no concept of enjoyment at all, except among the poor. They, if one can trust passing glimpses of cheap excursions, have the knack of having fun. But the better-off English, so far as I can see, seem totally unable to conceive of any pleasure beyond the ghostly satisfactions of doing one's duty. The phrase "sense of duty," as a matter of fact, takes the place of the ominous American "sense of humor," except that an Englishman described as having a sense of duty really does have one.

4. Our English acquaintances would be utterly incredulous if it were pointed out to them that they are consistently and unendurably insulting to Americans, but it happens to be true. As always, one must make a distinction in favor of the so-called lower classes, who, if they do not regard being an American as a pleasant and interesting attribute, at least succeed in giving that impression. But the

people we meet as equals have been trained from childhood to patronize Americans as Americans are trained from childhood to clean their teeth, and they do it just as automatically. They have been saying, as if it were the ultimate in compliments, "Of course, *you* aren't like other Americans" for so long that they are no more conscious of the affronting implication than they are of the chairs they are sitting on. There are luminous exceptions, of course, like Mr. Primrose, but generally speaking it is impossible for an American to get through an afternoon or evening in the company of English people without hearing at least half a dozen unmistakable hints that culturally speaking, his compatriots are running neck and neck with the anthropoid apes.

And however unconsciously and without deliberation these hints are thrown out, the effect on the visiting alien is disastrous. He can remind himself until he is blue in the face that the English would be more courteous to Americans if they were less desperately jealous of the United States, which is after all a tribute. It is, but it is not a tribute you would pick out if you had your choice of a better one. And the relentless and unceasing intimations of American inferiority, unimportant enough singly, have nevertheless a powerful cumulative effect. After a while you begin to find yourself as incapable of forming calm, unbiased judgements of England as a hay fever sufferer is of pronouncing with detachment upon the August countryside. It is not the criticism. Nobody with any pretensions to good sense objects to fair criticism. It is that the English do not criticise America for criticisable things. If they have ever heard of lynching, of municipal corruption, of the violence attendant upon American strikes, no syllable of reference to such shortcomings ever passes their lips. They have just one big blanket indictment of America. It isn't England. What can you do with people like that, except to go home and raise hell in a diary?

October 19th

Phyllis is as efficient as a train despatcher, and relations with her improve hourly. She is getting over the idea that she must, whenever she is in my presence, make her face look as much as possible like the façade of a conservative bank. She still puts on a double layer of impassivity for Henry, but when she hears him say anything funny, her eyes begin to blaze like something picked out by the headlights on a dark country road, though her mouth remains perfectly grave.

The social life of Yeobridge is beautifully paced. After a long, dreamy interval, one of the Yeobridge ladies invites me to tea. After another ditto, I invite her back. One moves up slowly, in Yeobridge, upon a social engagement and gets a fine long perspective on it during the approach. If the engagements are seldom worthy of such timing, at least the basic idea is sound.

The college, on the other hand, extends us so many invitations that if we accepted them all, we would be in Exeter every day from eleven in the morning till eleven at night. The college has grown away from the gentlemen-of-England tradition which fortifies Yeobridge and has not yet grown into any other, so that it clamors for sanction and approval. And, to be just, the college hospitality arises to some extent from greater kindliness and curiosity than is common to the gentry at Yeobridge. The college has been taken out of the refrigerator of the eighteenth century and left on the kitchen table. Naturally, it has begun to melt a little. Unfortunately—owing to that English spirit of compromise which sounds so sensible on paper and often proves to be a little disappointing and sloppy in actuality—the college confines its liberalism to its curricula and classrooms and committee meetings. At its teas and dinners we continue liberally to talk about the weather.

We went to tea at one of the hostels this afternoon. It was not one of the frequent, picayune little teas attended by people who give and take tea because they have forgotten how to stop. It was the rarer, big-gun tea attended by the Olympians on the faculty who think twice before they accept an invitation. I went fearlessly. Living in England is curing me with almost alarming rapidity of being shy. Even with the Olympians, there is no need to worry about appearing stupid, because it takes a great deal to produce ennui in an Englishman and if you do, he only takes it as convincing proof that you are well-bred. I have developed a splendidly meaningless smile and have worked up a handy reserve of vapid remarks, and there is not a village idiot for miles around who can hold his own with me. This, I believe (she said wickedly) is what Mrs. Northrup is referring to when she tells me I am not like an American at all.

The old classics teacher, the one with the beautiful, broken-down face that I admired last June, was at the tea and we had a long and stately conversation together. He paid me several Old World compliments which were extremely handsome, though they seemed to be based more on my discernment in having been born into the opposite sex from his than on any

197

qualities appertaining specifically to me. But he was charming, in his antiquated way, and very nearly had me exclaiming "La, sir!" and rapping him over the knuckles with my pocketbook, in lieu of a fan. I tried to remember not to be slangy, but before I realized it I found myself laughing and saying, "You have me on a split stick."

My companion opened his tired blue eyes very wide.

"What an arresting figure!" he said. "Do all Americans talk like that?"

Without waiting for an answer, he began to fumble in his pockets and eventually produced a pencil and a worn old red-leather notebook.

"Would you mind," he asked me shyly, "if I wrote that down?"

A few minutes later, when somebody else came up to speak to me, he wandered absent-mindedly away, tapping his notebook with his pencil and murmuring softly to himself, "Have me on a split stick, have me on a split stick. Dear me!"

I drank my tea sitting in a wide white window seat which commanded a beautiful range of the soft, misty Devonshire hills. The college Shakespearean shared the window seat with me. Henry speaks respectfully of the Shakespearean and says he is a far better scholar than he, Henry, is. I found him extremely entertaining. He was educated at Oxford, and an active mind, imprisoned in an Oxford education, makes the best of a bad thing by joking deftly about the prison walls. We talked about America. The Shakespearean brought the subject up. I myself am getting rather tired of explaining my native land, and especially of explaining it to people who have not the slightest intention of understanding it, if they can possibly manage not to. There were the usual references to Frigidaires and central heating. Oxford men, piquantly enough, do not ask about the Indians. One of the most surprising aspects of England— of Devonshire, anyway—is the extent to which the fate of the American Indian has captured that not easily capturable thing, the English imagination.

I had what the Victorian novelists used to call mingled emotions about the Shakespearean. He is witty, and his sentences circle and sing through the air like a lariat in the hands of a vaudeville cowboy, but the manner in which he said he rather liked Americans provoked me into answering bluntly, "You don't like them at all. But you think it doesn't hurt to play with them if you wash your hands afterwards."

He laughed for so long that I was hard put to it to find something to do with myself in the interval.

"Not at all," he said finally, "not at all," in

the soapy, gratified voice of one who denies a soft impeachment.

The last part of the tea I spent standing over the fire talking with Dr. Peters. Dr. Peters is the Peck's Bad Boy of the faculty. He was intended by Providence to be a British Tory, but he is flying in the face of heaven and trying to make a radical intellectual out of himself. The poor man has all the machinery of an intellectual (the books, the attitudes and the vocabulary), but not juice enough to run it, which makes him bad-tempered. The faculty wives say in admiring tones that he is "very bitter" and "a complete cynic," a reputation he earned by not troubling himself to answer their invitations. However, I must have caught him in a good mood today, because when he talked to me, he said he liked to stand on the side lines of life and observe people—nothing harsh or unkind, you know, but men and women are so interesting. I had looked forward to Dr. Peters. English conversation is so much like the English landscape, and even the Oxonian jokes are so full of resignation, that I had thought a little savagery would come as a pleasant change. Well-a-day. In these parts, apparently, a skeptic is a man who refrains from cuddling kittens.

October 22nd

Phyllis cooks so well that sometimes it is hard to believe we are living in England. Our diet is somewhat repetitious, but that can scarcely be avoided in a place where the wealth of Croesus could not buy any other vegetables than Brussels sprouts, cauliflower and cabbage. And at least we are not called upon to maneuver suet and treacle puddings through our exotic American alimentary tracts. How Phyllis manages her output of roasts and apple tarts and soufflés is more than a casual observer can tell, for she cooks on an ancient coal range with pronounced manic-depressive tendencies and a top so small that you cannot get two pans on it at once unless you brace one of them against the adjoining wall. Sometimes I look thoughtfully at Phyllis and wonder whether she ought not to be fastened into a niche and have candles burnt in front of her.

October 23rd

Mrs. Wadhams came over this morning to ask if she could get me anything from Exeter. She brought her baby with her. His face is just an ordinary baby's face, but he has his mother's coloring, except that his hair is silver- instead of yellow-gold and he is even more petally than she. According to Yeobridge folklore, Mrs. Wadhams rode to hounds until she was eight months pregnant, a departure from conservative notions of prenatal care which, if somewhat startling, is certainly justified by the results. A handsomer batch of protoplasm than young

Wadhams I have never seen. Mrs. Wadhams
herself, however, says that he looks like a Com-
munist, which seems to be a puzzling combination of a joke and the affront direct.

In Yeobridge, all left-wingers, however hesi-
tant and tentative, are carelessly and laughingly
classified as Communists. (The Russian Communists are referred to with airy familiarity as
"the Bolshies," the mere phrase being considered a smashing witticism.) This attitude—
though it seems, to say the least, childish and
impertinent—is nevertheless more endurable
and less bloodcurdling than the epileptic trans-
ports of American small-town reactionaries. Toward people with whom they disagree, the
English gentry, or at any rate that small cross
section of them I have seen, are tranquilly good-
natured. It is not *comme il faut* to establish the
supremacy of an idea by smashing in the faces
of all the people who try to contradict it. The
English never smash in a face. They merely refrain from asking it to dinner.

While Mrs. Wadhams was here, I asked her
what drawing a cover means. The careless as-
sumption of English novelists that a person who
can read at all must *ipso facto* be familiar with
the procedures of hunting has always fallen on
barren ground so far as I am concerned. To me,
a hunt is merely a rapid procession consisting
of first a fox, then a group of intelligent dogs,
and lastly a concourse of rather less intelligent

people. From Mrs. Wadhams, however, I learn that a cover is a piece of woodland about the size of a large pasture. Drawing it means introducing therein a pack of foxhounds who run around and paw and sniff and snort and make themselves as objectionable as creatures can who come by it instinctively. The fox, if there is a fox, then takes to his heels (thereby bringing a regrettable but necessary element of common sense into the proceedings).

The cover having been drawn, and having produced a fugitive quarry, the pack goes off pell-mell after the fox, and the riders, who are called the field, go after the pack. A furious hegira is had by all. The foxhounds work entirely by smell, so sometimes the fox can "steal away" from the cover unobserved or, if he is being chased, can suddenly contrive not to smell very much, so that the pack loses the scent and the fox gets away. In this case the huntsmen cheerfully shrug their shoulders and if there is time, they go and draw another cover. If the pack does not lose the scent, the whole assemblage belts along for twelve or fifteen miles. What happens then I do not know. I suppose suddenly they all find themselves on a Tiffany Christmas card.

October 24th

Mrs. Hayes calls me up almost every day with financial propositions whose laughing insolence nearly causes me to drop the telephone. She suggests that I should buy up all her old drawing room curtains so that she can get new ones, or take ten gallons of cider off her hands (at double what it costs in the village store), or buy six tickets to a church play in some little hamlet twenty miles off. It is a curious phenomenon and I am puzzled by it, for nobody appears to question Mrs. Hayes's gentriness and yet the rest of the Yeobridge gentry hold themselves frantically aloof from vulgar considerations of money and trade and bargaining. I decline the Hayes advances with whatever graciousness is consistent with an Everlasting Nay, but my refusals produce not the slightest alteration in Mrs. Hayes's manner. She gives me a little burst of mimeographed laughter, calls me a naughty girl, and calls up the next day for something else. I must ask Phyllis about her.

October 25th

I have been returning calls, an occupation which makes me realize with appalling accuracy what a diamond in the rough I am. I have learned that you leave two of your husband's cards and one of your own, though why I cannot tell, unless it indicates the relative status of men and women in England. I have even learned to judge how long fifteen minutes lasts without peering nearsightedly at the clock and sinking back with an eloquent, involuntary, "Oh!" But I cannot learn how to get rid of the cards.

Englishwomen leave cards in my house as unconcernedly as flowers shedding petals, but when I try to leave my cards in their houses, I have more trouble than if I were attempting to deposit a foundling. I endeavor first to give the cards to the maid who answers the door, but she puts both hands behind her and backs defiantly away. While she is announcing me, I look wildly around for a tray or a bowl, but if there is one, it is always hopelessly concealed under the strata of umbrellas, walking sticks, raincoats and garden shears that form an integral part of every English hallway. I suppose if you could find it, it would probably be fossilized. In the end, I am out on the doorstep again, saying good-bye and still clutching the cards—which by this time look as if they had been salvaged from the *Lusitania*—in my hot, unhappy palm. It always concludes by my having to hold them out and say, "Here. Here's something for you," as if I were distributing samples of shaving cream. One of these days I am going to find myself adding that there is absolutely no obligation.

October 26th

We have spent the evening with the Vinnicombes, playing records on their victrola. The victrola was a bitter disappointment. It must be ten or fifteen years old, and it transforms a string quartet into something that sounds like the horns of Elfland having a knock-down fight with a Diesel engine. But Mr. Vinnicombe had the scores, which Mrs. V. and I followed, and that made it enjoyable for me, since following the score seldom leaves me much time to listen to the music. Mr. Vinnicombe's scores are carefully marked out—codas, bridging passages, modulations and all—which made the quartets seem very lucid and architectural, though the victrola supplied only hints of their line and flow and you had to do the rest of that in your head. What a shame, I said to Henry afterwards, for someone like Mr. Vinnicombe to put up with that Iron Maiden, when good instruments are scattered so lavishly, not to say wastefully, all over America. But Henry smiled sadly and said that if Mr. Vinnicombe heard our victrola, it was not beyond the bounds of possibility that he would shake his head and say, "It isn't English."

You learn, after you have been in England three or four days, that when a Briton says, "It isn't English," there is nothing to do but pick up your hat and tiptoe quietly away. (Time out, to imagine Messrs. Brandt and Pedersen drawing themselves up and saying, "It isn't Swedish"!!) But, despite Henry, I acquit Mr. Vinnicombe in advance. When we had finished the music, he suggested whiskey-and-soda, not to Henry only, but to me, *moi qui vous parle*. In middle-class England a woman is offered a drink with the same degree of frequency with which she is offered deadly nightshade, and at English dinners, when it gets on for ten o'clock and you are numb with cold and half hysterical from hearing about English weather, the gentlemen all have whiskey-and-soda and the ladies, God bless them, have tea! A woman who wants hard liquor at an English dinner has to ask for it, and then her host (nice and warm himself, of course, in woolen clothes, long sleeves and the radiation from a quantity of port) glances questioningly at her husband, as who should say, "She's a little minx, but I don't believe a tiny bit would hurt her." It is a discouraging state of affairs, for (quite aside from the cold storage dining) probably no class of people in the world could do more handily with a little of the stimulation and release of alcohol than well-bred Englishwomen. However, a visiting American does better to refrain from proselyting, to do her drinking in large batches (if possible) on the maid's day out, and on other occasions to remain silent and stoically let the pleurisy fall where it may.

October 28th

I went, full of distaste for the whole undertaking, to call on Parse's Wife this afternoon and to my utter amazement, was received with great civility. The lady was, in fact, almost deferential. I could hardly wait till Henry got home, to report this astonishing change of front, but he was not surprised. Parse's Wife, he says, is an extreme case; but most of the English, while they like to tell an American (by delicate implication) that Americans are savages, like it even more if he declines (also by delicate implication) to accept the proposition.

October 29th

As a matter of cold fact, the barred clouds that bloom the soft-dying day come in the morning. At least, they do in Yeobridge. I wake up and see them, with the casement and the apple tree beyond the casement silhouetted against them, and it takes me several minutes to realize that they mean it is going to rain in half an hour.

The rain and the mail from the United States form our only contact with reality. The unhumanness of English social life, and the intensely far-off, antique and romantic aspect of Mrs. Turney's house and the country around it, make me feel that I am living, not in another country, but on another planet. I said as much to Henry at breakfast this morning. "I know what you mean," he replied sympathetically. "It keeps you wondering whether you have died or just not been born. And," he added, picking up the paper, "the London *Times* isn't much help in making up your mind."

November 1st

The hunting season opens today. A note from Mrs. Burton says the first meeting of the Yeobridge Pack is the day after tomorrow, and she and the General will call for me at half-past ten.

We have changed our newspaper subscription from the *Times* to the *News-Chronicle*. It was my idea that we should switch to the *Manchester Guardian*, which Henry reads occasionally in the faculty common room at the college, but we need a morning paper to read at breakfast and the *Manchester Guardian*, for reasons best known to itself, does not get to Yeobridge until late in the afternoon. That is, it would not, if anybody took it.

The *News-Chronicle* has a liberal slant and a rakish Scripps-Howard manner, and after the grave unreasonableness of the *Times*, it is like a breath of fresh air. I liked the *Times* at first. It seemed so big and solid and dignified; and its habit of putting cricket scores and poultry notes on the first five or six pages, before indulging in any political news, gave it an air of self-restraint and stern reliability. But after five months or so, its Latinized style grows very wearing, and nowadays I cannot even see a copy of it without having a vision of rows and rows of top-hatted reporters sitting at their desks and trying desperately not to begin their articles,

"What time the Ministry of Transport submitted its report. . . ."

"Sing, Muse, the Mr. George W. Blenkinsop, of Little Murfle, Berks., who on Tuesday last murdered his ailing helpmeet with an axe . . . ."

November 2nd

This evening a young man from the paper factory, sent by Mrs. Northrup, came to arrange for Henry and me to visit it. The young man, name of Higginson, is Doing Very Well and is intensely conscious of the fact. He wore a black, pin-striped suit, badly fitting, and a high, white, intensely clean collar. There was an awkward fervency about the Higginson collar, as if Mr. Higginson had only just discovered collars, and had fallen in love with the idea. He admitted, with a sort of rhinestone modesty, to great prowess in the Accounting Department, and when he spoke of the factory, it was with wonder and gratitude and solemn awe. I think if he had been standing up, he would have made a genuflection at the mention of the company's name.

When I asked him about accidents and compensation (he stayed for well over an hour), he glanced at me as if I had made an unwarranted error of taste and scrambled away from the subject. We are to meet him at the factory a week from Tuesday, when to him, a sinner and all unworthy as he is, it will be vouchsafed to show us the works.

November 3rd

General and Mrs. Burton called for me this morning and we drove to the neighboring village of Compton Regis, where the Yeobridge Pack was meeting. Leaving the car in a narrow lane, we walked to the public square. In the center of the square about thirty people were stamping around on horseback. Nearly half were women, many of whom—including Mrs. Wadhams—rode sidesaddle. A massive wedge of skirt covered the sidesaddlers from waist to ankle and they appeared to be sticking to the horse's floating ribs by some interesting combination of centrifugal force and capillary action.

The square was solidly lined with children, shopkeepers, grooms, and retired military men who conversed in short, cryptic barks with General Burton. Against this fringe of humanity horses plunged and reared until I thought at least half the onlookers would be trampled to death. But this frightful prospect did not seem to disturb them, and they even appeared to enjoy having hoofs down their necks. Three of the huntsmen were wearing white breeches, brilliant red coats and black velvet caps. Why, in English novels, are hunting coats always mentioned as being pink? Is this one of the more flamboyant examples of British restraint? One of the Redcoats bestrode a horse which was submerged to the knees in a swirling mass of dogs. The dogs, dirty white with large black and brown spots, had ears like old pillowcases. Curiously enough, though they were never still, they kept solidly together, so that they all moved as a unit, but slowly and wiggling at the edges, like an amoeba.

The riders tightened their girths. Another Redcoat took up a collection—to pay the farmers, the General said, for any wire that got broken by the huntsmen. I said humbly that I should have thought it would be the huntsmen that got broken by the wire, but the General only answered, "Yesyes," as if I were wasting his time with trivialities.

There was a perpetual stir in the square, but nothing seemed to be going to happen, so after a few moments I ventured to ask who pays for the dogs.

"Hounds," corrected Mrs. Burton kindly.

"NEVER call them dogs," said the General.

I opened my mouth to re-phrase the question

212

and a horse backed into it. I flung myself behind the General. "Take it *away*," I said. The General gave the horse a familiar poke in the buttocks. "Won't hurt you," he remarked casually over his shoulder. I resumed my place again. Mrs. Burton patted my arm and the General began to explain some of the fundamentals of the hunt. One of the local gentry keeps the hounds and either hunts them himself—in which case he is an M. F. H.—or pays a Master to hunt them for him. In either case, he hires in addition two or three "whips," who, like the Master, wear red coats and who take up collections and watch for the fox when he comes out of the cover. Those of the neighboring gentry who can afford to keep horses, pay an annual subscription to the owner of the pack—three pounds in Yeobridge, where the country is hilly; ten pounds in the Midland Counties, which are flat and fashionable.

At this point a big brown barrel moved into my range of vision and I looked up and saw two forefeet and a flushed Mammoth Cave of a mouth suspended in the air directly over my head. "Killed in a hunting accident," I thought, while the horse pawed at my temples. "It will make a nice high-class obituary." I had a momentary flash of a smiling red-faced man twenty feet above me who did not seem to know or care that he was about to indulge in manslaughter.

Then the horse shrewdly realized that he could not climb a tree, because there was no tree there, and he came resignedly back to his normal posture—clearing my cheek in the process by an eighth of an inch.

"You were saying . . . ?" I remarked faintly to the General, and Mrs. Burton looked at me proudly.

Further explanations were prevented by a great clatter of hoofs as the Master swept out of the square on a carpet of hounds, and the field rattled after him. We followed on foot. In less than three minutes the field was out of sight. This made the whole business seem pointless, but the General is not one to be interested in girlish misgivings, so I said nothing. At the edge of the village we came to a hill which I estimated roughly to be three miles high and which rose at an angle of ninety degrees. The General pointed to the top. "Ought to be able to see from there," he said. I looked at him to see if he were joking and found that he was already fifty feet ahead of me. We climbed. The road was six inches deep in mud and would have given pause to a drunken marine in a caterpillar tractor. A fine rain began to fall.

"Hey," I called to the General. "It's raining.'

"Good thing," he said, looking back. "Keeps the scent down."

By the time we reached the summit my legs

felt like a mess of spaghetti, but the grass was soaking wet and there was no place to sit down. Below us in the valley the field waited at some distance from the cover, while the Master and the whips patrolled the edges. A chorus of mellow howls arose from the woods. "They've found the scent," said Mrs. Burton. I was surprised at the melodiousness of the sound. In the ordinary way, it would not occur to me to look for madrigals from fifty dogs in a state of expectant agitation, but the noise that came up from the valley had a musical tenor quality and was like the clamor of bells.

We had a long wait. The rain continued with unassuming persistence and in a little while we all looked like something that had gotten tangled up in a paddle wheel. Anyone coming along, at that point, with a cup of coffee and a sandwich could have had me drudging for him for the rest of my life. The General said that since it was the first meet of the year, the fox was probably a young one which had never been hunted before and did not know that he was supposed to run. After several seasons a fox grows so polite that he turns around and says "Yoo-hoo" to the pack whenever they lose the scent, but in his first season he is apt to be a little gauche.

The Master and one of the whips were conferring and in a minute or two the whip rode into the woods, apparently to slip the fox a note from the Rules Committee. Whatever he meant to do, he did it successfully, for the next moment three foxes burst out of the cover. The peaceful little valley boiled like a battle scene. One of the foxes tore across the fields and nearly knocked down two small boys who were standing in a public footpath surveying the proceedings. The boys screamed lustily. The second fox raced toward a neighboring farm, and all the farm people (who had been watching the hunt) started scrambling up haylofts and trees and chimneys trying to see where he went and howling "Tallyho!" (presumably) with every second breath. The third fugitive whizzed past the Master and went up toward the brow of the hill opposite us, the hounds pelting after him. The Master roared out an infuriated "Tallyho!" and blew maniacally on a little horn. But the field had deserted him. Some of them had started riding down the little boys and the rest charged the farm and were nearly out of sight before they realized the hounds were not with them.

The General was writhing. "Sheep!" he agonized. And the Master's fox was indeed flickering up the hill, headed for a flock of sheep, the hounds after him, the Master after the hounds, and the rest of the field belatedly spurring toward the bottom of the hill. The fox flashed through the sheep and I lost track of him. The hounds stopped short when they got to the sheep and began snuffing fruitlessly around like a man trying to find a stamp in a hurry when his wife is away. "It spoils the scent," Mrs. Burton said, "if he runs through sheep." The field surged up the hill. Suddenly the hounds picked up the trail again. They gave tongue and were off over the crest of the hill, the riders after them.

"May as well go home," said the General sadly. "Can't see anything more."

It seemed to me an anticlimactic end to the business, but I was glad to call it a day. I was so thoroughly wet that I almost flowed down the hill and I wondered if I would have to keep on going till I reached my own level.

"What happens," I asked the General, "when the hounds catch up with the fox?" Mrs. Burton looked disturbed and then glanced at her husband to see if he had noticed. But the General was still wistfully trying to see over the brow of the hill where the hunt had disappeared.

"Tear 'im to pieces," he answered absently. "In a minute. Messy business. Rather."

"They really are a nuisance," Mrs. Burton put in, in her soft voice. "Foxes. They do a lot of damage. And they can run very fast," she added hopefully. "Quite often they get away."

After tea this afternoon I went out to get some cigarettes. I met Mrs. Wadhams riding slowly home from the meet. It was raining hard.

217

She was as splashed with mud as if she had gone
ten rounds with an avalanche. When she nodded
to me, a pint of water rolled out of the brim of
her hard hat and plumped into her lap.

"Did you get him?" I asked.

"He ran over ploughed fields. Spoils the
scent," she explained, and laughed. "Had a
jolly good run, though." She paced sedately off
through the downpour. "Glorious," she said
over her shoulder.

November 4th

Today was Phyllis's afternoon out and, thinking I was doing her a favor, I washed up the
supper dishes. But when she came in and viewed
this job lot of benevolence, she swept into the
drawing room with so much impetus as to forget her usual delicately respectful pause at the
door. "Adam mustn't *do* such things!" she said,
in such an agony of shame and embarrassment
that she instantly made me ashamed and embarrassed too, from sheer contagion. Henry
calmed her down with mild assurances that in
the United States perfectly irreproachable
ladies sometimes wash the dishes—a statement
which, coming from him, she seemed to regard
as authoritative. Lord knows, I am not a cur-
tain-fancier, and my interest in Lares and Pena-
tes is something short of absorbing, but it occasionally gives me qualms to observe the

artling contrast between my idleness and
Phyllis's industry. Phyllis, however, apparently
as no qualms at all. Quite the opposite, in fact.

November 5th

I spend a great deal of time talking to Phyllis,
whose bashfulness dwindles apace before her
delight in having a virgin audience for all the
old Yeobridge gossip. Phyllis's uncle is the sex-
on of Yeobridge's sixteenth-century church;
Phyllis's father runs the butcher shop; Phyllis's
aunt owns the bakery; Phyllis's cousin works in
the garage; Phyllis's sister is beloved of Captain
Wadhams' groom; and Phyllis's best friend is
the maid at Mrs. Pennard's. There may be one
or two harmless and spindling little microbes
which manage to move around Yeobridge without its coming to Phyllis's ears, but they must
have to go on tiptoe.

For the communication of local tidbits,
Phyllis (or perhaps Mrs. Turney had something
to do with it) has worked out a tangential tech-
nique. She would not dream of saying bluntly,
"Have you heard so-and-so?" Instead, she confines herself to making some completely ambiguous remark, usually when she brings in tea in
the afternoon. "I often wonder if Mrs. Pennard
knows it," she comments dreamily, setting
down the tray.

"Knows what?" I inquire helpfully.

Phyllis looks surprised, as if I had startled her from a half-slumber.

"Why, Adam," she says in a reproachful voice, "Major Keith-Hampton. He goes everywhere with Mrs. Pennard's niece, that lives in Compton Regis. And what I say is, does Mrs. Pennard know it? Because of course he's much too old for her." She pauses a second. "Though really," she adds penetratingly, "I think he's too fond of his own comfort to marry anybody."

Today I indicated circuitously that anything Phyllis cared to tell me about Mrs. Hayes would be received with appreciation. She looked at me as if I had just given her fifty thousand dollars, smiled, smoothed her apron, and went over the top. I was nearly lifted out of my chair by the spate of anecdote. Boiled down, it amounted to the fact that Mrs. Hayes is shamelessly and spectacularly parsimonious and, which is what Phyllis dwelt on especially, her treatment of servants is an intensification of the lines worked out by Pharaoh and the Egyptian overseers.

Well, well. I can hardly say I am taken by surprise. What I should like to know now is the effect Mrs. Hayes's avarice has on her social standing. The other gentlefolk do not mention it, but then, they are not great mentioners of anything, except it has to do with hunting or gardening or the weather or the evils of central heating. I can only suppose they endure Mrs. Hayes in stoic silence. Avarice, after all, is not adultery. It is not even "Communism."

Last night we had the Wadhamses to dinner, and not having the incubus of Auntie, it was gayer and less constrained than the evening we spent with them. Mrs. Wadhams looked beautiful—her head did, at any rate. I have read of women being just naturally pink and white and gold, but always assumed it was pure wishful thinking on the part of enfeebled novelists. The conversation at table began with Mrs. Wadhams and me chronicling, in a prettily rebellious manner, our husbands' deficiencies in carving. From then on the talk was taken up with ploughing contests, Red Devon cattle, pheasant shooting and Devonshire dialect. By dessert, the discussion had worked its way around to the kings of England. At the introduction of this topic, the Wadhamses assumed an air both modest and proud, as if we were talking about something rather fine which they had done, but which they had not intended to be found out. The attitude of the English, as a matter of fact, toward English history, reminds one a good deal of the attitude of a Hollywood director toward love. The Wadhamses, for example, think of the English monarchs as a series of dainty little fellows in velvet hats who never got into trouble because their hands were so full of falcons. If it were suggested in Yeobridge that James the Second (to take a random illustration) had catarrh and was a fluent spitter, the statement would be dismissed indignantly as being just the sort of thing an American *would* think of.

After dinner the Captain, warmed by port and lulled into security by the careful behavior of the Yankees, talked for a while about politics. All the gentry of Yeobridge are Conservatives, but the ungentry are Liberal and Devonshire is a Liberal county. The Captain had a sportsmanlike handshake for the Liberals, but only a cold nod for Labor. "A lot of discontented chaps," he said discontentedly. "Not cheerful." There was a gay reference to the Bolshies (laughter). A soberer reference to the miners of South Wales. The Captain assured us comfortably, however, that the miners sing remarkably well.

"For their supper?" I asked uncivilly, but the Captain was still talking and nobody heard me except Henry, who flashed me what is known in our household as The Unwisecrack Glance.

"You're wasting your time," he said mildly, after the guests had gone. "The Wadhamses have heard of social justice, but they think it means Winston Churchill handing out sixpence o a beggar who has had the good taste not to sk for it."

November 8th

Mrs. Pennard stopped in today to ask me if I would give a talk to the Women's Institute of Yeobridge next May. (Except for Mrs. Hayes, who must wear out three or four instruments a year, people in Yeobridge seldom telephone. They forget for weeks at a time that the telephone has been invented and resort as by instinct to notes or calls.) I had no good reason for refusing Mrs. Pennard, though at the very mention of public speaking my mouth goes dry and my mind feels like an old tube of toothpaste.

"What do you want me to talk about?" I asked in a manner the reverse of eager.

"America," said Mrs. Pennard dolefully.

"Well," I replied dubiously, "it's rather a large subject."

Mrs. Pennard looked as if she did not believe me.

"Hadn't I better take some single aspect of ?" I went on.

Mrs. Pennard pressed her lips together and the corners of her mouth went down like express elevators.

"Just America," she said in a mutinous quaver.

It rained very little in October and Devonshire was soft-eyed and lovely and full of subtle
ties. Now, though, the leaves are coming off the
trees and the garden begins to have an out-to
lunch look about it. The grass is still green, bu
it rains and rains and rains and rains and rains
Except for the drawing room and the kitchen
where there are fires, the house is icy-damp
with a dampness that cannot be warded off by
putting on more clothes, because the clothes are
damp too. Phyllis warms the beds with ho
water bottles at night. Last night she forgot to
do Henry's, and after he had slid into it, he
looked at me thoughtfully and said, "I think I'
rather be cremated."

Most of the Yeobridge gentlefolk have visited
the paper factory at one time or another, and
derived great comfort therefrom. The factor
is a small one, planked down in the middle o
the English countryside, with trees and hedge
rows coming right up to the railroad siding. I
is a setup which pleasantly confirms the gentr
in their conviction that the plight of the op
pressed classes is greatly exaggerated. However
not much import can be attached to a manu
facturing plant in Devon. The principal indus
try of the county seems to be not paper or ever

224

(in spite of the pastures and sheep and red cows) grazing, but providing a haven, very beautiful and rather cheaper than the rest of England, for retired military men and the relicts of the clergy. Though half-dissolved little Devon has hardly any other resemblance to Connecticut, there is about it the same proportioned, exquisite, useless air that Connecticut villages achieve when they have been taken over by well-off New Yorkers.

Inside the factory, the country-club-cum-museum note disappears immediately. We went first through a hot, steamy, unbearably smelly place where South American grass was being boiled up into pulp, and then we followed the pulp through an endless series of moving belts, all of which looked exactly alike to me, although they were not supposed to. The floor around the belts was splashed with puddles, some of them over my instep, and the factory hands wore shoes with soles inches thick. Mr. Higginson went with us, but the workmen explained the processes and Mr. Higginson had little to say. Some of the workmen were young, with bright blond hair and extremely red cheeks, and some of them were seamy and intensely middle-aged, but they all looked deep-dyed English. They attended us politely but with a sort of cynical good humor; the factory has a great many visitors and the workmen know spurious enthusiasm when they see it.

Just as we were leaving, I saw two little boys sweeping an immense, dusty litter down a long corridor. They must have been fourteen, which is the age for leaving school in England, but they were small enough to be taken for nine or ten. They glanced at us apathetically and then went drearily on with their sweeping. Their faces were almost blotted out with fatigue and they moved like sick old men. I touched Mr. Higginson on his pin-striped sleeve and asked him how many boys of that age were employed in the plant, but either he did not hear me over the noise of the machinery or he pretended not to. There is a curious distinction, incidentally, between English and American conservatives. It lies in their hearing. If an American reactionary has his attention called to subhuman living conditions, he answers with great heat that those people spend all their money on radios and fur coats. The British Tory, on the other hand, smiles radiantly and replies, "We *have* been having frightful weather, haven't we?" That is the principal difference, I think, between the two civilizations—Americans make an unconscionable noise and clatter in their running away from life, whereas the English have been running away from it for so long, they do not even know that it is there.

Talking to Phyllis tonight, after we got home, I mentioned that we had had to climb two dangerously dilapidated flights of wooden stairs at the factory. The treads were worn away to mere rungs and the structures wobbled perilously even under Mr. Higginson's insignificant weight.

"Don't they," I asked Phyllis, "have factory inspectors in Devonshire who report on things like that?"

Phyllis looked satirical, which is a thing one would consider impossible from seeing her face in repose.

"Oh, yes," she said drily. "The company gets summonses. But they never have to do anything about them."

I should like to find out whether Phyllis is right, but I hardly know how to go about it. If I asked the Yeobridge gentry, I should only be taken gently by the arm and led with consummate politeness back to my paper dolls.

November 13th

A long letter from Mr. Primrose, splendidly undisappointing. Clearly, he is having a good time, though he suffers horribly from the hot rooms and judging by his account, expects to come back to England clad in nothing more than a spoonful of gravy. But he notes with surprise and pleasure that an English accent goes

227

a long way in America (which is not exactly the fate of an American accent in the Stepmother Country), and though he left England to the accompaniment of loud choruses of his country-men exclaiming that he would not be able to stand the pace in New York, he says he likes the pace. He likes the music in New York—he thinks, as Henry does, that there is more of it and it is better than in London—and he likes American food and American coffee. Between his English and American students he notices the same differences that Henry does. And about the things he does not like, he writes calmly and rationally and without a single trace of It-isn't-Englishness.

Lovely, human Mr. Primrose. He is the only person we have met in England not in the "lower classes" who actually seems to be alive. Some of the more advanced Englishmen are interested in vitality, and they examine it curi-ously and kindly—leaning down for the purpose from a rarefied height where there is none. Most Britishers, however, from our experience of them, are not only not interested in it, but when they meet a person who has some, they promptly penalize him for offside play.

November 15th

Mrs. Northrup's brother—a consul some-where in eastern Europe, though I have forgotten where—is home on his vacation and this afternoon Mrs. Northrup gave a tea. It was a sizeable tea, and included a number of people from the villages around. I met the consul, a large, bald man with pink cheeks, faded blue eyes, and a white moustache of such dimensions that I expected the Maid of the Mist to emerge from it at any moment. Afterwards I talked for a while with the Vinnicombes. In their timid way, the Vinnicombes ask sensible questions about the United States, which is a great relief after the prevalent central-heating-Frigidaire-Redskin type of inquiry, even though I often cannot answer the Vinnicombes nearly adequately. I like the Vinnicombes, and I think they ought each to have a little aureole for not telling Henry and me, with a generous air, that they never think of us as Americans. But the poor dears are so exquisitely shy that even if they were our compatriots, it would take four or five years to get to know them and, being English, they probably require a lifetime of cultivation before they cease to look at you as if begging you not to be too frightening.

One way or another, the Vinnicombes and I got detached from each other and I subsequently talked to Mrs. Northrup for a while. Mrs. Northrup was in a state of distress because some of the men she had asked had not been able to come, at the last moment, which threw the male-female ratio out of balance. I condoled with Mrs. Northrup, and then I listened to Mrs. Pennard explaining abusedly that she had to leave early for a committee meeting. Parse approached me, bringing with him an unidentified woman, to whom he introduced me with a great flourish. "A temporary parishioner," said Parse, waving descriptively at me, and then stopped—undecided, apparently, which word to repeat. "Temporary," I suggested helpfully, but Parse had already given up and begun on a more tractable sentence. Eventually I found myself standing in back of a sofa talking to Captain Wadhams about the weather. Below me, on the sofa, were the consul and Parse's Wife.

". . . from Warsaw," I heard the consul say with business-like politeness.

"Warsaw." Parse's Wife's mind was not on what she was doing. Her eyes skated over the room. Then she leaned forward suddenly with a roguish smile. "Do tell me," she said, "where is Warsaw? I'm awfully afraid I don't know."

"Poland," replied the consul, in a flat voice. Parse's Wife sat back.

"I quite agree," she said soothingly, "I quite agree," and then I had to turn quickly back to the Captain, who was two showers and a cloudburst ahead of me.

Just before we went into the dining room for tea, I was introduced to a Mrs. Weatherby, who had come in late. Militant, dominating, Lars Porsena of Clusium bundled into tweeds, that is Mrs. Weatherby. When I was presented to her, she remarked grudgingly, "Hoddyadew," and then looked coldly at my hair and distastefully at my dress. I, meanwhile, surveyed her face and decided that should she ever have the misfortune to fall over on it, it would probably bury itself in the floor and remain there, quivering. I had hoped for a Vinnicombe at tea, but Mrs. Northrup led me up to a chair next to Mrs. Weatherby. "A wonderful woman," whispered Mrs. Northrup indulgently, indicating the Egdon Heath of Mrs. Weatherby's back. On my other hand, I had a thin, spidery creature whose name I had not caught, but whom Mrs. Weatherby called Grace. Grace and Mrs. Weatherby began immediately to talk across me as if I were not there.

Grace, when she speaks, pulls her lips up into a bunch around her teeth, as if she were afraid they would catch cold—which, considering their wanton prominence, is probably a shrewd precaution. She enunciates with rococo exactitude.

"The vicar was saying," she began, evidently picking up the threads of an interrupted conversation, "only the other day, that with all . . . due . . . respect . . . , he *must* say how sweet Queen

Mary is." She exhaled yearningly. "I thought it so nice of him."

"When I lived at Windsor," said Mrs. Weatherby in a loud voice, "we saw the Royal Family every Sunday. On their way to church." She lowered her tone mystically. "When you get close to them that way, you know how simple they are."

I looked about me. Little conversations had sprung up all around the table and were raging like brush fires, but I was hopelessly islanded.

"Such a splendid example for the lower classes," Grace continued, the languid rapture in her voice consorting oddly with her finicking speech. "Though perhaps the Duke of Kent. I always feel he's not quite so sensitive."

"The Royal Family are all sensitive," replied Mrs. Weatherby curtly. "I saw it when I was at Windsor."

"Oh, I'm sure, I'm sure," said Grace apologetically.

I spent the rest of the tea in a kind of trance. I ate scones, because there was a plate of them just in front of me, I drank my tea and I heard, like Ocean on a western beach, the surge and thunder of the Weatherby. There was, I recall, a long and exceedingly dogmatic reminiscence of Queen Victoria's Jubilee. "My dear, the crowds!" exclaimed Mrs. Weatherby in triumph, as if crowds were hard to come by and no other nation had ever had any. Here I lost the conversation for a while, for the two matrons were converging more and more closely on me and I experienced some difficulty in steering my teacup first past Mrs. Weatherby's bosom, which was almost on my plate, and then past Grace's teeth, which were in such proximity to mine that once or twice I very nearly made the mistake of putting my scone into her mouth.

As I finished my tea, Victoria's Jubilee was giving way to Victoria's Funeral. Over the Funeral, Mrs. Weatherby grew so *exaltée* that I thought for a while she was going to have the impressionable Grace shouting, "Hallelujah!" I wanted more tea, for scones are too dry to eat alone, but short of boring a little tunnel through one of my captors, there seemed no way of getting any. Shortly after this Mrs. Vinnicombe, who was opposite Grace, leaned across the table and told her gently and suggestively that I had taken Mrs. Turney's house. Grace looked at me and then at Mrs. Weatherby. Mrs. Weatherby's countenance could have passed in broad daylight for a Siberian tundra. "How interesting," said Grace and returned to the oracle.

"I remember Edward the Seventh's Coronation," she volunteered to Mrs. Weatherby. "Of course," she added with emphasis, "I was quite a little girl at the time."

"Humph," said Mrs. Weatherby skeptically.

I felt a stir of sympathy. If Grace was quite a little girl in 1902, then somebody has been using her in the interval to wipe off windshields with. Grace, however, ignored the skepticism.

"We were no further than that," she went on, waving at the sideboard, "from Kaiser Wilhelm." She wrinkled her forehead judicially, and when she spoke again, it was with a grieved and pensive accent. "You know, I didn't really care for him. He tried to manage things too much."

A clatter around the table roused me and I saw that Mrs. Pennard, at the other end of the room, was preparing to leave. I ducked low and slid out from between my two ladies. Grace looked at me in surprise. Mrs. Weatherby said accusingly, "Oh! You're going, eh?"

"No," I answered politely, "I haven't been here at all."

But Mrs. Weatherby had already forgotten me.

"Edward the Seventh . . ." she began sonorously.

Grace tittered.

"*He* wasn't sensitive," she said.

Mrs. Pennard and I stood on the doorstep saying good-bye to Mrs. Northrup. I took off my hat and rubbed my forehead. A headache was supposedly the cause of my defection, and I was brought up on admonitions that if a thing is

234

worth doing at all, it is worth doing well. But
the gesture was lost on my companions, for just
then a stentorian voice floated out of the dining
room. It informed us that if we had lived at
Windsor, we would know how sincere they are.
Mrs. Northrup looked fond and tolerant, and a
little flicker of the same emotion hung like a will-
o'-the-wisp over the marsh of Mrs. Pennard.

"She's so loyal," said Mrs. Pennard. ("This
time," I thought, "Mrs. P. really is going to
break into tears.")

I came to with a start and realized that both
women were looking at me.

"Oh," I said, "I'm sure, I'm sure."

November 16th

Henry is in bed with a cold. He has two colds
every winter, one some time before Christmas
and one after. He calls them Hänsel and Gretel.

Later

I have been looking at Henry propped up on
pillows and marveling at how little difference
there is between Henry well and Henry ill.
Even when he is in the best of health, his pallor
and his thin cheeks give him the air of a man
quietly bleeding to death and politely saying
nothing about it, and when he is ailing, he
merely grows a notch or two more pre-Raphael-
ite. When I explained this to him, he glanced

up at me from under his eyebrows and said, "It's the tight lacing that does it."

There are times when living in England makes you feel, momentarily, that back in New York you never really had any adequate idea of comfort. It gets dark now around four o'clock, and I take a last look at the racing clouds and the sodden garden and the solitary red rose thrashing hopelessly around in the wind, and then I draw the curtains. Henry, if he has come home early, pokes the fire. Phyllis brings in tea, in a silver teapot, and Henry and I sit around the hearth eating toast and strawberry jam and wallowing in well-being.

It occurred to me today, as I sat stirring my third cup of tea, that this relaxed, late-afternoon atmosphere extends over a good deal of English life. An American living in England is constantly fetching up with a whang against the caste system; against a corrosive envy of the United States; against the worn-outness of an old country; and against that death-in-life which the Britons, with characteristic understatement, like to call English reserve. In the irritation resulting from these collisions, the American tends to overlook the fact that he can read his English newspapers in the relative peace engendered by an absence of race riots,

lynchings, Vigilantes, rackets, wholesale mur-
ders, police brutalities and Roman holidays like
the Hauptmann execution. It is not, I think,
that the English are more fair-minded than
other nations, but that their unfairness is so
placid. British injustice is a leisurely inequity,
arrived at by due process of law and free from
any hoyden impulses to take people out and
string them up on trees. A good deal in England
makes the blood boil, but there is not nearly so
much occasion as there is in America for blood
to run cold.

November 19th

Hänsel has virtually gone, and Henry went
to Exeter this morning. He was back, however,
five minutes after he had left, with eight or ten
small boys. They were waiting for him at the
garage, he said, when he went up to the village
to get the car, and as soon as he appeared, they
exclaimed in chorus, "Uh've yuh got unny
stomps, Mister?" He put them all into the car
and brought them back, except for one small
creature who said he could get there faster by
walking, and did. I asked them to come in and
wait in the hall, but they only smiled at me
indulgently, as if they did not mind my not
knowing any better, and continued to stand on
the doorstep. We hunted out all the American
stamps we could find, and when we came back

with them, the boys began to giggle and stretch out their hands. But I noticed with surprise that there was no pushing and shoving, though the outer boys strained desperately on tiptoe. It was hard to distribute largesse fairly to that forest of waving hands, and some of the suppliants got more than others. But the unlucky ones only shrugged their shoulders philosophically and laughed without rancor. One of the boys accidentally got a big wad which I had meant to divide up. He glanced at the stamps, glanced at me, grinned wisely and started edging unobtrusively down the path to the gate.

"That's all," Henry said with finality, and there was a momentary silence. The visitors looked as if they knew they ought to say thank you, but could not quite get organized to do it. They shuffled their feet, smiled foolishly, and then suddenly bolted in a unit down the path and scattered, yelling, up the street.

November 21st

Mr. Primrose warned us in his letter that just about the time we are packing up next June to leave England, we will begin to get the hang of Exeter and Yeobridge and to discover which people we would really like to know. I begin to realize how right he is and how mistaken I was to think that living in England for a year would give one an idea of English life. English life is seven-eighths below the surface, like an iceberg, and living in England for a year constitutes merely an introduction to an introduction to an introduction to it.

November 23rd

Henry brought two of his students, a boy and a girl who had been helping him correct papers, home to tea with him this afternoon. My heart bled for them. The poor creatures were in such an agony of bashfulness that it would have been an act of mercy to turn them away at the door. Henry and I worked over them furiously with various kinds of conversational respirators, but it was not until five minutes or so before they had to leave that they began to show any signs of returning life.

These two were more than ordinarily shy, but there does seem to be a much wider chasm between students and faculty at the college in Exeter than there is in American colleges. They meet, apparently, only on the most formal social terms. I think the breadth of the chasm is due to the fact that youth has so little prestige in England. So far from being considered an enviable possession, it is regarded as something to be gotten over as hastily and inconspicuously as possible. "Experience" is the thing, and a person is said to be experienced who has spent forty or fifty years decorously avoiding experiences.

Nevertheless, I cannot help having the most wholehearted admiration for the manners of English children and the what seems to me sensible way in which they are kept in a separate department and not allowed to interfere with adult life. It is too bad that they emerge into adolescence hamstrung with shyness, but as the scarred and bitter victim of a series of New York children who are being reared (or rather, who are carefully not being reared) according to the dictates of progressive education, I could not help having a guilty appreciation of English upbringing even if the English elected to keep everybody under the age of twenty in chains.

I do not like those little American boys who come rushing into the room when I am visiting their parents and interrupt an otherwise enjoyable conversation by snatching the ice from my highball and putting it down my neck. I like it still less when (after the ice has been retrieved and the little boy has waggishly dropped it back into the glass) I arrange my face and mind to accept an apology as gracefully as may be, and the little boy's mother gives me a fond and secret glance and murmurs reverently, "Isn't it marvelous? He isn't the least bit shy." Not to mention the little boy's father supplementing her

Salad days in Paris

with a hearty, "I'm really not a partial parent. That kid's got poise."

Some day, I suppose, I am going to be pushed down an elevator shaft by one of these pocket-edition Calibans—and his father and mother will smile with a tender pride as they explain to my mourning relatives that it was part of a project in gravitation.

This, says Henry, is hitting the nail below the belt, and would certainly alienate all my parent friends if they heard me express it. Me, I do not think so. Nobody agrees with you more completely when you deplore the bad manners of modern children, than a set of modern parents. They never think you mean *their* children.

November 24th

Henry gets three weeks' vacation at Christmas. It is tacitly understood that we cannot afford to go away and it is also tacitly understood that we are going. Henry plumps for Paris, where, in his salad days, he once lived for several months, but I find myself with what is apparently an inexcusable deficiency of enthusiasm for Paris. Perhaps I have not read enough books, or perhaps I have not read the right ones, but the discreditable truth is that I am not interested in Paris and I want to go somewhere where there is sun. It has rained steadily for three weeks and this house is gradually turning me into a pond lily.

November 26th

Henry says—and though it startled me at first, I believe he is right—that in a way there is much more intellectual freedom in Yeobridge than there would be in an American small town. Henry's point is that in America small-town neighbors hurry to find out what one thinks and often indicate rather oppressively that it damn well better be what they think, whereas in Yeobridge nobody tries to find out what we think because it has not occurred to anybody that a well-bred person thinks at all.

November 30th

Mrs. Pennard—to tell me lugubriously that the Women's Institute speaker for December is unable to come, and would I mind . . . ? For once, I felt I could match Mrs. Pennard lugube for lugube. The talk seemed so faint and unhurtful way off there in May, but now it is to be December 15th. Henry says I had better be thinking what I want for my Last Meal.

December 1st

Henry has brought me a little book about Paris, which I am setting dutifully about to read.

Mrs. Wadhams came over today to borrow our fish kettle. She had young Wadhams tucked under her arm as if he were an extra coat. I thought he would have been justified in a strongly phrased protest, but he hung there quietly, only wriggling a little and looking reproachfully out at the world from under his dome of forehead. There was a big bruise over his eye. "He fell off the sofa," explained Mrs. Wadhams with a carefree laugh.

In return for the fish kettle, I exacted some information about the Women's Institute, which is, it seems, a national organization for brightening up the lives of rural women—farm women and village women. Theoretically, it is not run by the gentry for the poor, and theoretically, women of all classes participate in it on equal terms. But I note that the officers of the Yeobridge chapter are all gentry, and nobody, this side of delirium, could imagine a village woman having the temerity to get herself elected to preside over Parse's Wife, or even Mrs. Wadhams. However, the bulk of my audience will be farm and village women, who, for all I know of their tastes and capacities and limitations, might as well be so many Patagonians.

Mrs. Hayes's telephone calls have been tapering off lately, and I began to hope that she was getting the idea. But she called me up this morning and asked, strangely enough, if I would like to come over and see a bonfire. My indifference to bonfires, circuses and department store Santa Clauses could be hitched up and made to run a dynamo, but I felt so pleased and gratified and friendly that she had not asked me to buy anything, that I went. I found Mrs. Hayes dressed in what she laughingly called her "gardening clothes." They were garments of such surpassing antiquity that I decided Mrs. Hayes's principal function in a garden must be to frighten the birds away. I think she frightens them. Her coat alone would turn them white overnight.

When I came in the garden gate, my hostess ran up and quickly slipped a burlap apron over my head. My initial good will was slightly impaired by annoyance, and I was also perplexed. I could not understand why viewing a bonfire should necessitate my looking like a rose bush done up for the winter. But the mystery was cleared up the next moment.

"The gardener is so frightfully busy," Mrs. Hayes explained gaily. "I knew you wouldn't mind helping."

"HELPING!" I said. But Mrs. Hayes only laughed and pushed me down a muddy path. At the end of it was an eight-foot mound of the soggiest vegetation I have ever seen outside a goldfish bowl.

"I build a fire on *this* side of the pile," she said, "and you build a fire on *that* side. The inside is really quite dry, and if you get a good heart of ashes, you can burn anything."

I came to a halt in front of the mound and looked at her. I had no rubbers on, and I was wearing kid gloves and a blue Cashmere sweater which I bought in London last summer and to which I am profoundly attached. Mrs. Hayes avoided my glance.

"Here are some twiggy bits," she said, ramming me in the chest with a mass of dead thorns. "Just crumple up those newspapers and put this on top. I'll do the same over here, and then I'll let you light them both. Young people always like that," she added indulgently.

Presence of mind is a thing even the most favorable critics do not claim for me. I had a very distinct idea that the way to make this bonfire a success would be to have Mrs. Hayes tied to a stake in the middle of it, but I went meekly to work making my fire, through sheer inability to cope with the situation. Presently the fires were built and I touched a match to each of them. Mrs. Hayes's fire ducked into the bottom of the mound and began burning steadily in a modest but industrious fashion. My conflagration promptly went out.

"What a pity," said Mrs. Hayes with what was definitely maternal solicitude, but whether for me or the fire I could not tell. "Have some more twiggy bits." She picked up another armful of thorns, but I jumped nimbly away and she had to put them on herself. Then she darted back to her own fire, and in a minute called me to help her. Thick yellow smoke was pouring out of the top of the mound and in Mrs. Hayes's section the flames were licking through the side of the pile. "Cover up the flames," said Mrs. Hayes urgently and darted up to the pyre with an armful of drenched vines. I picked up a dripping stick covered an inch deep with mould and laid it tentatively on the fire. Then I retreated to a little hummock of grass which stood up above the general wallow of mud. Mrs. Hayes made no comment on my withdrawal. She had seized a pitchfork and was shoveling sodden weeds from my side of the pile onto the burning sections. "Heart of ashes," she said in my direction. "When you get a heart of ashes, you can burn anything." She worked vigorously for ten or fifteen minutes. I had abandoned all pretence of cooperation and stood silently apart, brushing sparks off my sweater, wiping smoke out of my eyes, and batting viciously at floating embers. Finally Mrs. Hayes thrust her fork into the ground and came over to me.

"It's too bad about your fire," she said con-solingly. "You didn't have enough twiggy bits."

"No," I said.

A little tongue of flame crept through the thick rolls of smoke and Mrs. Hayes plunged away. She pasted the flame with a thick coating of vegetable slime, and then came back to me.

I made a sudden decision.

"I have to go home," I said.

Mrs. Hayes looked surprised and a little hurt.

"Well, of course . . ." she answered. "I hoped. . . ."

"I have to go," I said tenaciously. "Letters to write."

Mrs. Hayes sighed.

"Duty before pleasure," she replied, with a brave, understanding smile.

I fought my way out of the burlap apron.

"Good-bye," I said resolutely. I looked at my gloves. The twiggy bits had reduced them to a mere fringe around the wrist. Mrs. Hayes watched me with her smile half turned on.

"Don't let anyone tell you,"—I mustered what courtesy I could and waved toward the burning bush—"that you'll never set the river on fire."

Mrs. Hayes thought for a minute, and I turned toward the path. Then she laughed.

"If you have a heart of ashes," she called after me.

I woke up this morning to as fine a piece of weather as I have ever seen—dew on the grass, leafless trees pricked out against a blue sky, and the sun shining quizzically on the holly berries. The Wadhams groom came clattering down their driveway with the Wadhams horses, and the sound of hoofs punched lively, satisfying holes in the still, pre-breakfast silence. In England one rapidly gets over the extravagant American habit of ignoring the weather for hours at a time, no matter how good it happens to be. Good weather here is so rare, and the countryside—satisfactory even in the rain—is so altogether disarming in the sunlight, that when there are two or three hours of unequivocal clarity, you drop everything and give them your closest attention.

December 7th

I have been studying the little book on Paris, but it does not do you much good to read a gargoyle-by-gargoyle description of Notre Dame when you do not have it in front of you.

December 8th

The ordeal by Women's Institute makes me realize how little I know of the village women. Except for seeing them in the streets and stores or when they come to the house to deliver bread and milk, I have no contact with them. Phyllis, tireless in botanizing the gentry, dismisses the villagers with an impatient gesture, as being too familiar and too hopelessly stodgy and unenlightened for discussion. The sum total of my knowledge of them is:

1. That some of them live in picturesque cottages which are dark and damp and have vermin in the walls and others live in ugly red-brick houses which are not dark and damp and do not have, etc. Most of the village people get their water by the pailful from a faucet in the public street.

2. That Mrs. Pennard "visits" the villagers, apparently to remind them (in case they have forgotten) that it is their duty to be happy in what the Prayer Book euphemistically calls "that state of life to which it has pleased God to call them." These visits seem always to result in acute dissatisfaction on either side, but both parties recoil in horror from the idea of discontinuing them.

3. That the gentry speak of the villagers with good-natured contempt, until the villagers reach the age of ninety, which they all do. When they are ninety, they become "characters" and are referred to enthusiastically as Old Jenkins or Old Mrs. Jenkins. A

ninety-year-old villager, in fact, is almost on a par with a Simple English Girl.

4. That in spite of the cheerful readiness with which they exchange greetings when you pass them, they are so reserved that I sometimes wonder if they would not have brought a speculative gleam into the eyes of Madame Tussaud. Village reserve, nevertheless, is distinctly different from gentry reserve. Gentry reserve has panic intensity. You sense the startled fawn underneath. Village reserve seems to have nothing underneath. It just goes all the way to the bottom, like water in a pond.

December 10th

We are going to Paris for Christmas, I having given in because Henry seems to have his mind so set on it, though I cannot get over a feeling that Paris will have wide, bleak streets and be full of oil paintings of onions. A craving for sunlight is taking large bites out of my morale. It need not even be warm sunlight, so long as it is bright and dry. The Devonshire weather, though not cold, is unendurably damp. Against his unheated classrooms, Henry has bought a kind of underwear he calls his quarter-inchers. I walk furiously to keep warm, and when not walking, I live in a six-foot semi-circle in front of the drawing room fire. Every time I go into the bedrooms, I wonder what our chances are of winning through to the spring without beginning to look like Roquefort cheese.

December 12th

Phyllis and Henry have come to my rescue. Henry suggests that I limit the Women's Institute talk to a comparison of Yeobridge with, say, some New England village I happen to know, and Phyllis contributes the equally sensible idea of comparing only the kinds of things with which the village women are familiar—houses and streets and gardens and churches, etc. Now, at least, I have something to go on, and if I could only manage not to get an attack of rigor mortis the moment I am looked at by more than one person at a time, I should be able to take the Women's Institute in my stride.

December 13th

Winter weather in Devon has a soft, womanly tempestuousness about it. It rains, and the wind is wild and wet, but not biting. The fields are green—some of them (planted, I think, with some sort of winter grain) vividly so. Occasionally, in the lanes, a bird sings. The hedgerows look less solid and more wreathy than they did in the summer, but the stiff holly and ivy leaves have a dark sheen and the abundant holly berries—this is a good year for holly—take the seriousness out of them. The wind makes creaking and scraping noises in the hedgerows, but overhead in the trees it makes a soft, remote roar, like the sound in your head when you go under ether. Clouds drive across the sky all day long as endlessly, but not so neatly, as holiday traffic on a through road, and sometimes they come down so low that the hilltop trees get blurred with mist. Altogether, a submissive kind of winter, temperate and English and not likely to get out of hand.

December 14th

I have been selecting my reading from Mrs. Turney's library, which is mostly Dickens and Thackeray. Thackeray reads just the same as he always did (which, so far as I am concerned, is very well), and having seen England since I last read him makes little difference. But Dickens, read in England, seems much funnier than he did in the United States. I suppose it is because Dickens's characters are unequivocally English, whereas people like Blanche Amory and Beatrix Esmond and Becky Sharp have a streak of American outlook in them. In fact, the inhabitants of Yeobridge, I believe, would be glad to give us Becky Sharp, in return for one Red Indian in good condition.

The modern part of Mrs. Turney's library is made up of the English "somehow" writers—

those gentle, misty-eyed, pipe-smoking artists
whose hearts are in the right place and whose
brains are there too; and in whose placid, dog-
cart-infested books nothing ever happens exactly, but always "somehow."

December 15th

The Women's Institute talk was accomplished
in something akin to the third stage of anaes-
thesia and was perfectly painless after all. When
I arrived at the W. I. building—a rectangular,
stuccoed structure on the main street—I was
steered by a tongue-tied and sheepishly smiling
village woman into the auditorium. The auditorium is small, old-fashioned and woodeny-
looking and across the footlights of its narrow
stage stretched an array of pink and red-and-
white-striped flannel nightgowns, spread out to
display their imposingly voluminous cut.

Before this unclassic frieze Mrs. Burton presided uncertainly at a deal table which confronted forty or fifty village women, with Mesdames the gentry in the back row. I suspect Mrs.
Burton of having submitted to election only because it was urged upon her that Mrs. Northrup
and Mrs. Pennard could not in decency be presi-
dential perennials of too much hardiness.
Shrinkingly, she let fall her gavel. Mrs. Pennard read the minutes of the last meeting in her
Fifth-Avenue-bus-in-second-gear voice, and I

had just time to realize that the room was un-heated and approximately as habitable as the bottom of a well when I found myself on my feet in front of the nightgowns.

There was a sound of rasping, half-choked utterance and I thought with detachment, "There's a woman with a seagoing larynx," not realizing for several seconds that it was I. After that, however, the talk spoke itself. The notes and outlines which I had typed out and pecked at and ultimately torn up, rose from the grave and made themselves manifest. I merely stood by and listened, noticing absent-mindedly, meanwhile, the extreme politeness of the audi-ence and wondering idly whether every eye was fixed on me because I was mesmerizing the listeners or vice versa. In no time at all it was over and I was sitting on the side lines again, huddling up in my coat and hoping anxiously that the meeting would come to a close before some shiver of tidal wave proportions jerked me right off my chair. I wondered remotely what kind of impression I had made, but it did not seem particularly important.

The ensuing reports of tag days, etc., were more or less what I had expected of the agenda, but I was surprised to note that the village women seemed to be getting some of their own back. In Yeobridge a lady is supposed to in-terest herself in the poor, though Phyllis claims that no one in the village is what she calls "really poor" and that anyone who wants work can get it. Nevertheless, a lady has a certain quota of soup which she takes to aged field hands and a certain quota of energy which she puts into the Girl Guides. It is part of the pattern. And I noticed at the meeting that the gentry were working devotedly—reporting, announcing, planning, and wheedlingly trying to coax the stolid villagers on to committees. But the villagers were not working at all. They sat back and contented themselves with placidly accepting the activity and attention as if it were their natural right. There was, in fact, a slightly regal air about them. I realized that I must, for them, have been simply one of the laboring gentry.

The meeting ended in a burst of prize-giving, most of the awards going to village women. Parse's Wife, however, won three shillings for growing the most potatoes on one plant. She gave me a bright, significant look, seemingly intended to indicate (lest it should have escaped my attention) that she did not care anything at all about the money, but was generously pretending that she did in order not to disillusion the humble folk. Mrs. Hayes won a prize for giving the largest number of uses for left-over bread. A faint, faint smirk drifted across the faces of the ungentry.

After the prize-giving, we had tea with the milk already in it, thick bologna sandwiches, and Pink Cakes. Pink Cakes seem to be more or less inevitable at an inexpensive English tea, whether restaurant or institutional. They are disastrously sweet and they have little silver pellets sprinkled across the top. The pellets look like—and judging from internal evidence, probably are—ball bearings from roller skates. During the tea I stood in the center of the room accepting the polite congratulations of the gentry, while the village women clustered in the corners and eyed me with shy, curious glances. When I went home and Henry asked me how it had gone, all I could say was that they had sat very still. But Henry says perhaps Phyllis will come across.

December 16th

Phyllis has come across—and, in fact, seems to be taking a possessive pride in my venture. As the village people come to the kitchen door on their customary calls, she brings word into the drawing room that so-and-so thought the talk "very nice"—beamingly laying the compliment at my feet like a generous puppy which has just dug up a delightful old shoe. I half suspect Phyllis of achieving these verdicts by threats of withdrawing our trade. Phyllis's aunt even went so far as to say that Adam's eyes sparkled *so*, which impressed Phyllis as a singularly acute piece of criticism and came as a great surprise to me, for I remember they felt like bits of isinglass. At any rate, the job is over and done with and I am not likely to hear anything startling or revealing about it one way or the other. Here in Yeobridge life does not dare come any closer than arm's length.

Day after tomorrow we go to Paris.

December 17th

I have been rearranging books, and I am hot and dusty and my fingernails feel bent back. Henry brought a packing case of American books with him from New York, thinking that the first thing required of him at Exeter would be a course in American literature. But the subject was not mentioned, and when he suggested it himself, the Shakespearean quickly smothered him in a whirl of sunny appeals and charming evasions which proved, on cold analysis, to amount to a statement that there is no American literature and if there were, nobody would want to read it. Oh, well. As Henry points out, we like the feel of English life, with its leisurely, cream-of-mushroom-soup texture, so we must not complain when we have to pay for our rest cure with sharp bursts of self-control.

257

LONDON—I have bought Henry a leather cigarette case for Christmas and I send him out of the room at intervals, so that I can take it out and fondle it. London, a dull enough hole in which to buy things for women, has things for men which are likely to give you trouble with your saliva. Henry has bought some ties and a new hat—though this latter, it is my private opinion, was a waste of money. Henry always drops his hat down first and then throws his coat on top of it, so that it takes him no more than two or three days to make a brand-new one look like a half-eaten pie.

Christmas does not seem to be the glittering, rather orgiastic affair in London that it is at home. The Bloomsbury hotel at which we are staying has put some pink and green streamers across the ceiling of the lounge, but the rooms are so cold that I sometimes wonder whether I ought not to plant a flag and claim them for the United States—a speculation which interferes noticeably with the seasonal cheer. The big stores have gotten out a few amateurish trimmings that look as if they had already seen hard wear. Otherwise, there is little to indicate the approaching holiday. The servants at the hotel do not affect the hothouse jollity of doormen and elevator boys in New York during the week

258

before Christmas. The English people who wait on you have a pre-Christmas manner all year round, the darlings.

December 20th

PARIS—But this is wonderful! We crossed by the train-ferry, and the Channel was smooth as a rug. Arriving in Paris this morning, we left our bags at the hotel, which is on the Left Bank, and went to a café called the Deux Magots for breakfast. There was hot chocolate so rich and beautiful that I had to keep pushing the calories back into the cup with my spoon, and from then on I stopped thinking that I needed sunlight.

At the end of one day in Paris, where I do not even know the language, I feel more at ease than I ever have in England. It is not only being warmed with wine and good food and central heating and not having to breathe coal gas and the smell of cabbage. It is that Parisian women go in at the waist—a thing which, living in England, you are apt to forget that women can do. And the people in the cafés look as if they were talking of things they were interested in and knew about. In England, discussing any subject on which you are well-informed is called "talking shop" and is bad manners. English conversation is distributed beforehand on multigraphed sheets, and when you come to the end of the sheet you go back to the beginning and start over again. Our long winter's nap in Devonshire has its points, but it is exciting to be back in the world of men again, where people have blood and brains and stomachs, not to mention various other convenient devices.

December 21st

London, with its alleys and areaways and juttings and recessions and general brownish tone, is Dickensian; but Paris is suave and Thackerayan. The wide boulevards and grey, uniform, impersonal house fronts make Paris look like a well-shaven jaw. In point of handsomeness, it does not begin to compare with Stockholm, Paris being half hidden under a landslide of broken-down, flatulent classicism. The public buildings are so ribbed with columns they look like washboards stood on their sides, and pediments are as much in evidence as poppies on Decoration Day. But Stockholm, for all its sleek design and fresh paint (in Paris, nobody gives a damn about paint), seems an old sobersides of a city compared to this alert, perceptive, humorous place.

December 22nd

We have been talking about how to spend Christmas, and have decided to go to Chartres

—this alert perceptive place

Christmas Eve and hear the midnight mass in the Cathedral. Henry's Christmas present to me is a bathroom. That is to say, we are doing things in style this time, and our hotel room is a big red chamber which might very well have come out of a bagnio designed to catch the trade of the Diplomatic Corps. It has its own bath, a large, grey, mirrored apartment which, if it would not quite do for the signing of a peace treaty, would at least suffice for a trade agreement or a defensive alliance. The concierge at the hotel is exceedingly amiable to us. He is a stout little man with snapping eyes and a moustache which makes him look like Birnam Wood on the way to Dunsinane.

December 23rd

Henry tells me, rather wickedly, that the things we are seeing and doing are the regular tourist things to see and do in Paris, but I am having too good a time to be bullied with words like "tourist" and "popular."

December 24th

CHARTRES—After the soft, abundant contours of England, the countryside between Paris and Chartres looks dismayingly gaunt and bleak. The trees are tall and skinny, like American trees; the farmhouses high and narrow and bony-looking; and the fields stretch flatly away into the distance without benefit of hedgerows. But if the countryside is comfortless, the hotel at which we are staying is just the reverse. It stands on a big, cobbled square, and has green shutters outside and white woodwork and flowered wallpaper inside. The atmosphere crackles with holiday abandon. Large, unwieldy family groups stand in the lobby saying *"Pourquoi pas?"* and *"Pas du tout!"* and using every muscle of their bodies to do it. In the bar an imposing Christmas tree has been set up and decked out with a competent lavishness. More families swarm into the bar, pronounce the tree *très gentil*, and then sit down and carefully order one cup of coffee apiece, which they nurse along so that it lasts three quarters of an hour.

The dining room was full at dinner time. Waiters skimmed prayerfully to and fro, corks popped occasionally, and the sound of voices hung like a cloud over the tables. Our table was next to the windows, and sometimes there was a provocative ringing of footsteps outside as people went past in the square. We sat relaxed and glowing over the dessert, and Henry said, "How would you like to spend Christmas in an English hotel?"

I thought of the piecrust and the cold rooms and the desperate handful of mute and stony Britons.

"Do you call that table talk?" I answered
coldly.

December 25th

Though the midnight mass was solemn, a
good deal of the joviality of the hotel seemed to
have seeped into it too. The chancel was brilliantly lighted with candles and electric light,
but the nave was in darkness. Almost every
seat was taken. A long double line of little boys
paced up the center aisle and entered the choir.
They wore scarlet robes and skullcaps and had
little scarlet capes, edged with white fur and
reaching to the elbow, over their shoulders.
They looked like baby cardinals. The choir
chanted, sometimes together, sometimes antiph-
onally. A sad phrase in minor kept recurring
over and over again. People came and went
continually, and in the side aisles there was a
steady rustle of whispering and of tiptoeing feet.
We were near the front, and in our vicinity a
middle-aged man with a weak, discouraged face
and a uniform like a British admiral's was fuss-
ing up and down the aisle. He was apparently
trying to regulate the incoming flow of wor-
shippers, but they all smilingly ignored him and
he padded wistfully around, stumbling occasionally when his long sword caught under a
prie-dieu and looking like a moth ball charged
with disciplining a plague of locusts.

263

A woman near me, dressed in heavy, un-equivocal mourning, dabbed at her eyes with her handkerchief from time to time. Another woman, handsome and dressed with distinction, was reading a novel. She tilted the book to get the light from the chancel and kept the place with her finger when she knelt to pray. In spite of the service which was proceeding splendidly in the chancel, there was a pleasant, help-your-self, cafeteria feeling about the nave, and when we had had enough, we rose unguiltily and went away.

Later

We have been to see the Cathedral by day-light. Henry had told me that the two towers of the western front were not alike, and I had my cautious, provincial taste all lined up to think the arrangement unpleasant. But a spiky and intricately decorated Gothic spire sharing the same building with a plain steeple does not look nearly so queer as it sounds. For a moment, to be sure, the façade suggests a man with a peg-leg standing on his head, but this irreverent fancy is no match for the authentic innocence and boldness of the building, and it quickly subsides.

It is a grey day, and inside the Cathedral the dimness was emphasized by the tapers burning in front of the images. Across this luxurious,

candle-lit twilight the stained glass windows
pulsed and rumbled with color. When we came
outside again, the daylight seemed a slack and
paltry thing to have been behind those kingly
ardors. Henry asked me if I knew the Gothic
spire was said to be the most beautiful one in
Europe. I said no, but that I was sorry to hear
it. It is exactly the opposite of inspiring, I think,
to be told that something you are looking at is
the most beautiful something in somewhere. It
takes your mind completely off the object in
question and sends it ranging hungrily over the
idea of a Society For The Suppression Of All
Statements To Which There Is No Possible Answer Except A Feeble "Really?"

December 26th

PARIS—We came back to Paris yesterday for
our Christmas dinner. Birnam Wood was glad
to see us again. I do not wear a wedding ring,
and this omission evidently gives Henry and me,
in Birnam's eyes, an air of jaunty self-indulgence
which he finds irresistible. Whenever we appear
in the lobby, he looks on us meltingly and says,
with an exquisite blend of wistfulness and approbation, "*Ah, la jeunesse! la jeunesse!*" Then I
say politely, "*Ah, la belle France, la belle France,*"
which is the only French I can trust myself to
pronounce, and we all three smile emotionally
at each other. After that, Birnam escorts us to

the door or the elevator, whichever way we happen to be going, with a flourish which implies unmistakably that doors and elevators are not available for the other guests, but are especially reserved for interesting transgressors like Henry and me.

We ate our Christmas dinner at Foyot's. It cost ten dollars and was the gastronomic equivalent of the stained glass at Chartres. There was a chicken in champagne sauce with mushrooms which made every other chicken I have ever had seem, in the recollection, like boiled albatross. After the dessert, Henry had the inspiration of ordering *crème fraîche* to put in the coffee. *Crème fraîche*, though indubitably *crème*, does not taste very *fraîche*, but at least it serves to modify somewhat the burned-ink flavor of French coffee. After having a brandy, we took a few turns along the river and then went to bed, feeling like a couple of impressionable children who had just celebrated their First Communion. When I reflect that I had in a manner of speaking to be brought to Paris by the scruff of the neck, only the matchless effrontery of the wedded wife enables me to look Henry in the face.

December 27th

I have a feeling that this diary is going to peter out after we get back to England again.

Henry has recently resurrected his textbook. Henry's textbook is a sort of Penelope's shroud; it always consists of three chapters. Once or twice a year, in a spurt of energy, he hunts it out and writes a few more chapters, but then it gets laid aside and while I am not looking, he unwrites it again, and the next time it appears there are still only three chapters. However, he says this time he is not just keeping the franchise, he is really going to finish it, and if he does, I will have a pretty collection of reading and typing to do. In any other place but Devonshire, that would not necessarily interfere with the sparse jottings of a diary, but in Devonshire time is so thick and measureless and muffled that just eating three meals a day and keeping partially awake between them is an occupation in itself, and anything further than that constitutes frenzied overwork.

December 28th

We are going to hear *La Bohème*, and this morning, while Henry was out buying English cigarettes (which I have learned to like better than American ones), I thoughtlessly rang for the chambermaid to take my evening dress to be pressed—forgetting, for the moment, that I am almost devoid of French. I studied it in school, of course, but all I remember of it is an Irishwoman we once had as an instructor who was a fervent baseball fan and who made us all go up to the board, when the Yankees won the American League pennant, and write, "*Les Yanks avaient battu le drapeau!*" When Henry returned, he found the maid and me confronting each other across the unmade bed, the maid clutching the dress and saying shrilly, "Kleent? Kleent?" and I fumbling desperately through a dictionary and saying with equal shrillness, "Wait a minute, wait a minute, pas de kleent. . . ."

"And Sheridan twenty miles away," said Henry pleasantly from the door frame, after which he came in and tossed the maid a wad of her native tongue which sent her away smiling a tucked-in little smile. Henry has an affinity for accents, and he goes right up to a foreign language and takes it by the halter and pats it on the nose, in return for which it leans down and nuzzles him fondly.

As for me, I can listen to the English You-Americanizing from now till Doomsday without having a single qualm of humility, but not being able to speak French really does make me feel like something which is likely to drop down on all fours at any moment.

December 29th

We walked in the Luxembourg Gardens this afternoon. They have no grass underfoot, only

268

greyish earth planted with rows and rows of trees—black and leafless now—in relentlessly regular order. The promenaders in the Gardens looked like ants which had gotten into one of those skimpy hygienic hairbrushes. Later we looked in at the Panthéon. The Panthéon, being a Hall of Fame, is practically guaranteed to be dull, and it is. It is dirty and classical outside, clean and classical inside. The large, cold interior is bare, except that the corners are filled with complicated monuments to Liberty, who usually appears as a naked woman being swarmed upon by a great many people who still have their clothes on. The misty, romantic Puvis de Chavannes murals of St. Genevieve look faded and cowed among all the rampant Atticism.

Going to Michaud's for dinner, we passed the house Henry stayed in when he came to Paris after leaving Oxford.

"What were you like in those days?" I asked, as we moved on again.

Henry gave me a sidelong glance.

"A scholar and a gentleman," he answered primly. "My wild oats weren't sown. They were raised in flowerpots."

December 30th

A subdued but ceaseless activity murmurs round the Venus de Milo, and singly or in little groups, people trickle unfailingly up to it. They look at it with curiosity from the front, but by the time they have moved around for a side view, they have begun to remember that it is a masterpiece. The scrutiny from the rear, now thoroughly self-conscious and unhappy, is followed first by a quick glance around to see whether anyone is watching and then by a studiously leisured departure. About one person in six turns around again, when he has gotten twenty feet or so away, for a final, painstaking stare.

On the benches nearby sit the sterner souls who are not afraid of masterpieces. A militantly haggard woman—English, from the hanged-by-the-neck look of her clothes—keeps her eyes on the statue as if she suspected it of an impertinent intention to walk away. Across the hall from the Englishwoman is an American girl. The American girl's tweed clothes sit on her in a manner which suggests that she dresses well because somebody takes an interest in her, and not because she cares about clothes herself. She hunches over a guidebook, and is evidently checking over the statue as it if were a pile of things just back from the cleaner's.

A guard walks past. He refrains, with something like deliberation, from looking at the Venus. A Frenchman comes up leading two little girls, young-old looking in their fashionable coats. The Frenchman regards the statue with a faint perplexity. The little girls look gloomily straight ahead of them. Enters, impetuously, a blonde young woman in tortoise-shell glasses and a shabby brown velvet coat, trailing after her a disconsolate and vacuous young man. The young woman stops precipitately in front of the Venus, and assumes the expression of a terrier to whom somebody has just said, "Rabbits!" Her escort adjusts himself spiritlessly at her side. After a moment the young woman thrusts one arm out in front of her and makes a sketching movement with her hand.

"The *lines* . . . ," she says.

Her companion remains silent and immovable, but into his eyes there comes the faint, sick look of one who is being shamed for the thousandth time and has every reasonable expectation of being shamed for another thousand. The other people around the statue, however, glance at the young woman with admiration, except for the tweed girl and the Englishwoman, who cooperate in a joint scowl of imposing dimensions.

The blonde young woman marches around to the side, where she tips her head back and squints at the statue with narrowed eyes.

"The *proportions* . . . ," she says, at length.

The tweed girl looks outraged and the Englishwoman stands up and flounces pointedly away. But the blonde young woman does not notice. The people around the statue are glancing at her respectfully, and one or two nod their heads sagely, as if "The *proportions* . . . ," were exactly what they had been thinking and they were glad to hear someone put it so succinctly. The blonde young woman strides exultantly around to the back. She is evidently preparing to deliver some comments from that position, but her escort, his face as unalive as a shopwindow at three o'clock in the morning, comes up and takes her quietly by the elbow. She starts, somewhat consciously, gives him an apologetic smile, and benignly allows herself to be led off.

The blonde young woman's audience drifts away, and a new assortment of people gradually accumulates. A small boy disentangles himself from a background of adults and goes up and touches the statue. An old lady says, "Oh!" in a horrified voice. The small boy looks at her coolly, flicks the stone again with his hand, and then turns away as if he had lost interest.

There is a sound of high heels chattering on the floor and two American women, very narrow of hip and very bulky with fur across the shoulders, come down the long corridor. They pause crisply in front of the statue and look at it as if they were trying to visualize it in a black satin dinner gown. After a short but intent survey, they relax and glance understandingly at

The Louvre

each other. One of them voluptuously shifts the fur on her shoulders. The other speaks in a sharp voice, with a note of delicate triumph in it.

"That only leaves the Mona Lisa," she says.

December 31st

The west front of Notre Dame seems to me much more English than French. The flat-topped towers and the great width in proportion to the height, give it a solid, spreading, down-to-earth impressiveness like that of the tremendous oaks and beeches standing in the fields around Yeobridge.

January 1st

Customarily I spend New Year's Eve having something really distinguished in the way of a rotten time. Ambiguous young men bump into me and ask me if my name isn't Horowitz, and before I have time to say no, they add hastily that they have always meant to call me up. But this New Year's Eve was cut on a different pattern. We went to hear *Bohème*. The voices were not particularly brilliant, though they were adequate, but the cast sang and acted with a Gallic verve which suggested that they were all just a little bit tight. It seemed to have just dawned on them what a youthful opera *Bohème* is, and they kept rolling it over and over on their tongues. The audience, too, was in a mildly vinous glow, and what with the appreciative impetuosity behind the footlights and the impetuous appreciation in front, it was a rosy, cosy, exciting evening.

Henry and I went back to the hotel afterwards to discuss a cold fowl, which we had asked Birnam Wood to leave for us. It was a tough and leathery little creature, and had the distinction of being the first inferior food we have had since we came to Paris. But we were overstimulated by the opera and were not hungry. We chewed down a few rolls and sat for a long time passing a bottle of Vouvray back and forth and conducting an increasingly benevolent conversation in which every sentence began with, "One good thing about you is . . ."

January 2nd

Henry wrote the rough draft of another chapter for his textbook this morning. He hates to write, only doing it because he likes having written, and the process of creation involves his smoking at twice his usual rate and almost wearing a groove to the bathroom. The unalluring truth is that his first drafts, at any rate (which is all I have ever seen him do), are not particularly well written. He has only one sentence—a long sentence, generally with a semicolon in the middle, and with participles sticking out like breasts. But he is unstingable under criticism, and only says sorrowfully, when I ask permission to cross out the fourth subordinate clause in a row, that I must have barber's blood in me.

January 3rd—Reduced for Clearance

1. The Botticelli murals in the Louvre look like May Day at a woman's college, only much more plausible.
2. The main difference, it seems to me, between England and Paris is that England looks comfortable, but is not, whereas Paris is just the other way around.
3. American men look at women when (they think) the women are not aware of it; Englishmen do not look at them at all; but Frenchmen look at them with such thoroughness and intensity that you half expect them to approach and ask dubiously, "Is it washable?"
4. Versailles is filled with thousands of tons of statuary—very neat, very white, and overwhelmingly reminiscent of coated almonds.
5. The Victory of Samothrace ought to be kept in England. It makes you want to pull in your stomach as you have seldom felt called upon to pull it in before, and that is a thing which a tourist in Paris is not often in a condition to do.

Serious-minded Henry warns fun-loving Peg that she will probably be sorry if she lets her diary trail off, on getting back to Yeobridge.

But the fact is, that I am losing the impulse to diarize. The impact of England startled me into making notes, but now—having resolved Yeobridge into the general working proposition that the countryside would melt in your mouth and the gentry will not melt in hell—I begin to slip back into laziness and silence.

The final day in Paris. We cross tonight. A last walk up the Champs Elysées. A last lunch at a small restaurant called Chez Doucet where other people's elbows creep in and out of your casserole and the clientele is subject to sudden, immense bursts of laughter. A last visit to the Cluny Museum which, having complacently allowed itself to get cluttered up with old iron-work and old wood carving and the gold-embroidered cloaks of sixteenth-century knights, is much more fun than the Louvre. The last lingering, sensual decision about where to have dinner.

I do not know what I would think of Paris if I knew it better, but I cannot imagine my present, violently tender regard for it being much modified. Some places and people evoke on the instant a fund of forbearance and resilience that is not available for other places and people, no matter how hard you try.

YEOBRIDGE—In the station at Paris, Henry, opening the door of our compartment, which he had closed in order to stow away the luggage, found himself more or less eye to eye with a feminine posterior big enough to be landscaped. It belonged to a lady who was leaning out of the corridor window saying good-bye to some friends.

Henry said something impulsively which I did not hear, and then stood clinging to the doorknob and looking supremely embarrassed while the owner of the rear elevation backed out of the window, straightened up, gave him a look of stately hatred, and coasted out to the platform of the car.

"What did you say?" I asked, when she was out of earshot.

Henry made a repentant grimace.

"I said I wished I had a thermometer," he answered.

This is the third time I have come into England, and I seem always to have the same reaction—an excited discovery, or re-discovery, of the countryside; a profound gratitude for everybody's peacefulness and good manners; and a feeling (arising from the amateurishness of the food, heating, lighting, stores and women's clothes) that I am just playing house with the kiddies and that in a quarter of an hour I will have to get back to the serious business of life again.

We reached Yeobridge in time for tea, and found a roaring fire in the drawing room and a flattering quantity of mail from the United States. Phyllis, in honor of our return, had cleaned up the house until it looked almost like a mirage, and timidly, and with a Big Bertha of a blush, she said she was glad we were back.

Some barely perceptible humps in the garden she says will be aconite, the first spring flowers; and the lambing season begins this month. Phyllis says Adam will enjoy the English spring. I think I will. Her manner was so primly authoritative that I would not dare not to. While I was out in the garden with her, she said absently, "I think there's going to be a baby there."

"Where?" I asked, looking around.

"Why, Adam," she said, in the tone of one addressing a wilful child, "at the Wadhamses."

Gentlemen, I give you the English Ungentry. The next time we come to this country, I hope Henry will get an exchange with a plumber.

ABOUT THE AUTHOR

MARGARET HALSEY *was born very quietly in Yonkers in 1910 and was sifted inconspicuously through the Yonkers public schools. She then went to Skidmore College, where she was very thin, very earnest and addicted to writing* "how true!" *in margins. She says that in the ensuing years she has become less thin, less earnest and no longer writes anything in margins because she has stopped reading anything except detective stories.*

In 1936-37, Margaret Halsey took an M.A. at Teachers College, but she has never taught. She has no children and one husband. Her hobby is not being photographed by candid cameras.